# PERMANENT JOB LOSS

and the
U.S. System of
Financing
Unemployment
Insurance

Frank Brechling
and
Louise Laurence

1995

W.E. Upjohn Institute for Employment Research
Kalamazoo, Michigan

**Library of Congress Cataloging-in-Publication Data**

Brechling, Frank P. R.
    Permanent job loss and the U.S. system of financing unemployment
insurance / Frank Brechling and Louise Laurence.
    p. cm.
    Includes bibliographical references (p. 103 - 104) and index.
    ISBN 0–88099–160–7 (cloth : alk. paper). — ISBN 0–88099–159–3
(paper : alk. paper)
    1. Insurance, Unemployment—United States—France.
2. Unemployment—United States.    I. Laurence, Louise. II. Title.
HD7096.U5B72    1995
368.4'401—dc20                                                    95–19352
                                                                       CIP

The facts presented in this study and the observations and viewpoints expressed are the sole responsibility of the authors. They do not necessarily represent positions of the W. E. Upjohn Institute for Employment Research.

Cover design by J. R. Underhill.
Index prepared by Shirley Kessel.
Printed in the United States of America.

# Preface

The research underlying this book has taken us many years. We are grateful for innumerable contributions and suggestions we received in a number of seminars. Specifically, we would like to thank Christopher O'Leary of the W. E. Upjohn Institute for Employment Research for his patience and careful guidance. We also acknowledge with gratitude the financial support for our research from the Upjohn Institute and the administrative support of the National Foundation for Unemployment Compensation and Workers' Compensation.

# Authors

Frank Brechling is professor of economics at the University of Maryland, College Park. Trained in Europe, he has held teaching positions at several European and U.S. universities, including the London School of Economics, Massachusetts Institute of Technology, and Northwestern University. His primary research interests are in labor economics. Currently he is on leave in Yerevan, Armenia, where he is setting up a research institute in economics.

Louise Laurence is an associate professor of economics at Towson State University. She received her Ph.D. in 1987 from the University of Maryland, College Park. Her past research has focused mainly on aspects of unemployment insurance financing. She has had articles published in *Applied Economics* and the *Quarterly Review of Economics and Finance.*

# Contents

# List of Tables

# List of Figures

# 1
# Introduction and Summary

The U.S. unemployment insurance (UI) system is unique in the world in that it is financed by an *experience-rated* payroll tax. This means that individual firms pay higher or lower UI taxes depending on whether they cause more or less unemployment—and unemployment benefit payments. Experience rating internalizes the costs of unemployment to individual firms, thereby inducing them to stabilize employment patterns. Hence, experience rating may lead to a reduction in layoffs and in unemployment.

Since the inception of the federal-state UI system in the mid-1930s, the experience-rating provisions have been vigorously debated among politicians, trade unionists, business people, and academic economists. The last comprehensive treatment of all aspects of experience rating was undertaken by Joseph M. Becker, whose seminal book on this topic was published in 1972. His views were restated, with minor modifications, in his 1981 monograph. Becker's work was followed by the contributions of Feldstein (1976), Brechling (1977), and Baily (1978). The early literature was surveyed by Hamermesh (1977, 1978), Gustman (1982), and Topel and Welch (1980).

## The Need for Research

In the research underlying this book, we have reexamined the role of experience rating in the UI system. Such a reconsideration is needed because of recent changes in labor market conditions, including the growth in *permanent* employment reductions due to major downsizing by some large employers, increased numbers of plant closures, and bankruptcies. Large structural shifts in economic activity and employment took place in the 1980s, and they are likely to continue. Thus, the question arises as to whether the present UI system and, in particular, its experience-rating provisions are capable of coping adequately with the consequences of the substantial reallocation of labor. Our research is aimed at providing some answers to this important economic and political question.

Current systems of experience rating seem to be well designed to allocate the costs of unemployment caused by temporary, easily predictable, and recurrent layoffs. Such layoffs do not lead to significant permanent employment changes. There are valid arguments for allocating the costs of temporary layoffs to the firms that caused them. Further, in most states, it seems that the existing experience-rating systems can be modified to allocate these costs to the appropriate firms.

Most theoretical and empirical investigations of the UI system have been based on models of temporary layoffs. For instance, the influential article by Feldstein (1976) and later contributions by Wolcowitz (1984) and Cook (1992), all employ an approach, similar to that of early implicit contract theories, in which employees have a lasting attachment to a particular firm, but are laid off periodically and later recalled in a fairly predictable manner. In these models, UI benefits are a means of raising workers' incomes during periods of temporary unemployment, and, so the argument goes, these benefits ought to be regarded as part of the firm's labor costs. If, by contrast, UI benefits were financed by a general payroll (or other) tax not based on an experience rating, there might be more layoffs, and high-layoff firms would receive a permanent subsidy from low-layoff firms. As a result, high-layoff activities would be expanded. Experience rating clearly leads to increased efficiency and social well-being, at least from a long-run perspective.

In much of the UI research, experience rating is modeled in a fairly abstract manner. For example, following Feldstein's original contribution, many researchers have described experience rating simply by the ratio of total benefits charged to the tax payments of employers. The reserve ratio method of experience rating, which is the most commonly used approach, has been modeled by Brechling (1977) and, more recently, by Wolcowitz (1984) and Cook (1992). Cook has extended the work to the benefit ratio method, the other important technique of experience rating. Both approaches imply that experience rating is imperfect in the sense that (1) there are substantial lags between the payments of benefits to workers and the corresponding receipt of UI taxes, and (2) there are maximum and minimum tax rates that curtail or even suspend the relationship between benefits and taxes. Although these features of the UI tax systems have been modeled in an insightful manner by both Wolcowitz and Cook, neither examines the effects of *permanent* employment reductions.

Suppose now that a substantial proportion of total layoffs is permanent, necessitated by some structural development, such as changes in tastes, new technologies, or competition from imports. Some plants may have to close completely, some may go into bankruptcy, and others may experience substantial downsizing. In any case, employment in the industry must contract substantially. From a social point of view, who should bear the unemployment costs of these layoffs? Is experience rating a desirable property of the UI system? Do present experience-rating methods allocate these costs appropriately? These types of questions have not been considered in the previous literature on experience rating. Consequently, we have addressed these issues in our research for this book.

## Study Results

Our work has produced a number of findings. First, permanent employment reductions amount to about 70 percent of total employment reductions. While employment reductions are not necessarily the same as layoffs, our evidence, using UI data for Texas for 1978-89, together with some previous results, indicates that permanent layoffs are a significant proportion of total layoffs. Thus, our analysis of experience rating in the context of permanent layoffs seems justified.

Second, based on our theoretical model, the socially optimal rate of moving labor from contracting to expanding sectors can be achieved only when the transfer costs are borne either by the laid-off employee or by the employer in the contracting industry. *The agent who pays for the transfer costs must also control the rate of transfer of labor.*

Wages and prices adjust to different payment mechanisms to bring about the same socially optimal rate of labor transfer. Even if wages are not fully flexible, the socially optimal rate of transfer may still be achieved by charging the costs to the employer in the contracting sector. Furthermore, under the current system, laid-off workers are paid UI benefits on the condition that they actively search for alternative employment. Although this requirement is enforced with varying vigor in the states, it is designed to ensure that workers are, indeed, transferred to the expanding sectors at a socially optimal rate.

When the agent who pays for the adjustment costs does not control the rate of layoffs or hiring, there tends to be a large, nonoptimal adjustment of labor, or high structural unemployment. Since the government is usually not able to control the rate of transfer of labor, payment of the adjustment costs by the government (financed, for example, from general revenues) is nonoptimal. It may be argued that government financing is justified, to the extent that markets bring about *too slow* an adjustment. However, we conclude that, in general, experience rating (charging the costs of unemployment back to the contracting employers) generates socially beneficial results. This conclusion reinforces the finding that, with only temporary layoffs, increases in the degree of experience rating tend to lead to improvements in the allocation of resources.

Third, when layoffs are permanent, payroll taxes are not an ideal way of implementing experience rating. Temporary layoffs leave the taxable payroll (that is, the tax base) more or less unchanged, while permanent layoffs reduce the taxable payroll. Suppose, for example, that a firm's layoffs increase and that the UI benefits received by the laid-off workers are charged to the firm's account. If the layoffs are temporary, the taxable payroll remains more or less constant, and tax payments increase after a lag. If, by contrast, the layoffs are permanent, the taxable payroll and, hence, the firm's tax payments fall immediately. After a lag, the firm's tax rate and tax payments may rise to reimburse partially the UI system. In the limiting case, when the firm goes out of business, its taxable payroll and tax liabilities fall to zero. Thus, the charged benefits can never be recovered.

Our analysis shows that, under both systems of experience rating, UI tax liabilities are less than the benefit costs of permanent layoffs. In particular, when the firm is and remains at the maximum or minimum tax rate, it receives a *tax reward* for laying off workers permanently. This is the very opposite result to that intended by experience rating.

When the firm's long-run position is on the experience-rated portion of the tax schedule and the maximum tax rate applies only temporarily, then the reserve ratio method of experience rating, because of its longer memory, tends to generate a higher ratio of taxes to benefit costs than is true with the benefit ratio method. In other words, the reserve ratio method tends to internalize a higher proportion of benefit costs than is true with the benefit ratio method.

We conclude this book with suggested economic policy changes. These recommendations are designed to increase the degree of experience rating and the degree of internalization of the costs of unemployment. Some of our policy suggestions have been made before: increasing or abolishing the maximum and minimum tax rates and shortening the lag between benefit charges and tax increases would improve the performance of the systems.

Our relatively new policy suggestions refer to the reserve ratio method of experience rating. First, positive balances in the UI trust fund should be treated as part of the employer's assets, and negative balances should be considered as liabilities. Second, upon bankruptcy, the firm's positive or negative balance in the UI trust fund should be counted as part of business assets or liabilities. Moreover, the UI trust fund ought to be allowed to claim reimbursement for part or all of the firm's UI liabilities in bankruptcy proceedings. Third, interest should be paid to the firm on its positive balances and charged on its negative balances. Together with the abolition of the maximum and minimum tax rates, these provisions could ensure the complete internalization of the costs of permanent as well as of temporary layoffs.

Much of the analysis underlying this study is abstract and mathematical. In our exposition we have attempted to present the arguments and principal findings first in intuitive terms and then more formally. We hope that this structure, which inevitably leads to some duplication, makes the research meaningful to a larger readership than would be the case with a tight mathematical presentation.

# 2
# Principles of Insurance and the Current Structure of U.S. Unemployment Insurance Financing

In this chapter, we sketch the background to the central analysis presented in the remainder of the book. First, we discuss briefly the major principles of insurance and the manner in which experience rating operates. Second, systems of unemployment insurance (UI) without and with experience rating are outlined and analyzed. Third, the two chief experience-rating methods currently used in the U.S. are described. We then briefly review some of the relevant recent theoretical literature on experience rating.

## Some Basic Principles of Insurance

Insurance is a contract in which an individual pays premiums to an insurer, who promises to compensate the insurant for a loss caused by some unpredictable circumstance covered by the agreement. Thus, insurance is a hedge against the costs of uncertain events. Risk aversion on the part of the insurant and the ability of the insurer to pool risks make insurance possible, likely, and generally efficient from an economic perspective.

Insurance may, however, entail some inefficiencies. Most notably, the so-called moral hazard problem arises when the insurant has some control over the insured event. For example, an insured business owner facing bankruptcy might hire an arsonist; if the owner could easily arrange for the burning of the business, insurers would be unwilling to provide insurance. Thus, for private insurance markets to exist, the insurer must be able to control moral hazard at a low cost.

In well-functioning insurance markets, the price of insurance, namely, the premium, is set at a level such that the present value of the stream of the insurant's premiums is just equal to the expected present value of the individual's insurance claims plus the cost of administering the contract, all measured over an appropriately long period of time. Insurants with similar risks of loss are grouped together into a risk class and are charged the same insurance premium. Thus, within a risk class, insurance claims and premiums tend to offset one another, both over time and across different insurants. In other words, risks are pooled both over time and among different members of the same risk class. As a consequence, over an appropriate span of time, the members of the risk class finance their own claims, producing neither a surplus nor a deficit. In any particular year, any member of the risk class may, of course, have a deficit or a surplus with the pool.

It follows that an insurant's weekly, monthly, or annual insurance premiums will differ according to the risk class to which that individual is assigned. For example, teenagers pay higher automobile insurance premiums than do adults, house insurance is more expensive for dwellings located near frequent mud slides or in a hurricane area, life insurance is more expensive for people with severe medical conditions, and so on.

In some types of insurance, in which the insured event occurs repeatedly, the insurant may be reassigned periodically to a different risk class, depending on the person's prior claims experience. This procedure is called *experience rating,* and it is particularly helpful when the factors, such as age, sex, and marital status, are not very accurate predictors of the insurant's risk class. Thus, if an insurant's claims were very low over a period of years, the individual may be assigned to a lower risk class with a decreased premium. In effect, the experience rating establishes a link between past insurance claims and the current insurance premium. Perhaps the best known example of experience rating occurs in automobile insurance in the form of "good driver discounts." Experience rating may also be effected through a special levy, such as deductibles or copayments, when an insurance claim is paid.

Two related aspects of experience rating are of special interest. First, experience rating implies incentives for the insurant to reduce claims by either controlling the uncertain events or by not submitting claims. Experience rating in automobile insurance may induce insurants to drive more carefully and/or to pay for minor accidental damage out of their own pockets, so as not to lose the "no claims bonus." In this way, experience rating tends to reduce the various forms of moral hazard in insurance.

Second, experience rating implies that there is participation by the insurant in the insurance against the occurrence of the uncertain event. This is the *coinsurance* aspect of experience rating. The extent of this participation depends upon the degree of experience rating. As the degree of experience rating increases, the insurant's premium (or copayment) corresponds more and more closely to his/her recent claims experience, so that the insurant pays more of the bill out-of-pocket.

Suppose, for instance, that the insurant has a claim for $5,000 and that consequently this individual's premium either shows no change or rises immediately by $500 or $5,000. If the premium does not increase, there is no experience rating. If it rises by $500, there is some degree of experience rating. If it rises by $5,000, experience rating is extreme in that the insurant suffers the entire loss. Since the total insurance premium includes a charge for administrative expenses, the insurant will reject contracts with such severe experience rating conditions: they impose costs (the $5,000 plus administrative fees) yet offer no insurance protection.

Experience rating appears to be particularly effective in discouraging relatively small and frequent claims against which insurants are quite willing to self-insure. Further, since these types of claims tend to have especially high administrative costs, their elimination is likely to reduce average insurance premiums.

### Experience Rating in Unemployment Insurance

Unemployment insurance (UI) provides a valuable service. If workers are risk averse because, while unemployed, they cannot borrow against the expectations of future earnings, then they are likely to be willing to pay a premium (possibly in the form of reduced wages) for insurance that mitigates the effects of income fluctuations. These individuals are willing to exchange an uncertain, fluctuating income stream for a certain and constant one with a smaller expected present value (see Baily 1977, 1978; Stafford 1977; Topel and Welch 1980; Rosen 1983; and Burtless 1990).

In spite of the persuasive arguments for this insurance, private UI markets have been very limited. Many reasons for this apparent market failure have been adduced. For instance, Rosen (1977) and Topel and Welch (1980) ascribe the deficiency to the high concentration of claims during recessions, which inhibits risk pooling among workers. Whatever the reason, all industrialized societies have seen fit to introduce public UI systems. In general, these systems are financed out of general government revenue or by a uniform payroll tax. Only rarely are taxes imposed on the individual insurants, namely, the workers.

As stated earlier, the UI system in the United States is unique in that it is financed by a payroll tax assessed on and experience rated for individual employers. Thus, employers owe higher taxes when the unemployment benefits paid to their laid-off employees are larger. Details of the two most common methods of experience rating are presented later in this chapter.

### *Simple Analytical Model of Unemployment Insurance*

To illustrate the major consequences of experience rating in unemployment insurance, we postulate a simple model that preserves the essential elements of the various arguments. Assume that there are two competitive industries, which are identical in all relevant respects except that one is stable and one is unstable. The stable industry faces a nonfluctuating demand, whereas the unstable industry is subject to recurrent demand swings that may be fairly regular (cyclical or seasonal) or random. Further, within the unstable industry, the demand fluctuations are distributed randomly across individual employers. In the short run, those employers are not affected identically by the variability in industry demand, but over a suitably long period of time, all employers in the unstable industry experience the same average fluctuations. Employers have the ability to mitigate the impact of swings in demand upon layoffs by means of production smoothing and similar techniques, which have marginal costs. Employers balance these costs against the costs of layoffs and rehires and thus determine their optimal layoff rates.

We assume that the total labor supply for the entire economy is not responsive to wage changes (that is, it is perfectly inelastic), although workers can move between the two industries. All workers are assumed to be homogeneous in the relevant characteristics, and, in particular, to have identical degrees of risk aversion. Movements of workers between industries are sufficiently responsive so that, in the long run, the net compensation of employees is equalized in the two sectors. Layoffs are effected by employers, without influence by workers and are distributed randomly across employees. Workers may have the ability to control the duration of unemployment, however, by accepting or rejecting new job offers. All of these assumptions can be relaxed without affecting the essential results of the following arguments.

We analyze this simple model under four different sets of circumstances. First, there is no formal UI system, so that employees must self-insure. This means that workers in the unstable industry must provide for their own income maintenance during periods of unemployment, by saving and/or borrowing. Second, there is private UI financed by premiums charged to individual workers. Third, there is public UI financed by a uniform employer tax. Fourth, there is public UI financed by an experience-rated tax. For the sake of simplicity, we assume that all UI programs are complete, in the sense that they smooth out completely the income fluctuations caused by layoffs.

### Self-Insurance by Employees

In the absence of any type of UI program, a reasonably well-functioning labor market would generate, at least in the long run, higher average earnings in the unstable industry than in the stable one. The absence of earnings during layoffs would be more than offset by high earnings during periods of employment: the average annual earnings in the unstable industry would have to compensate risk-averse employees for the cost and trouble to self-insure against the consequences of layoffs. Competition in the labor market would maintain this earnings differential.

Workers in the unstable industry would have an incentive to control their unemployment duration by accepting any alternative job offers leading to an increase in earnings. Similarly, employers in the unstable industry would have an incentive to control layoffs; if they could reduce layoffs at a sufficiently low marginal cost, they would be able to attract workers from the stable industry at lower annual earnings. Lay-off rates, unemployment duration, and earnings would be optimal, given that risk-averse workers must self-insure against fluctuating income, in the sense that all agents optimize by equating the appropriate marginal costs and benefits.

The allocation of resources between the stable and unstable industries would also tend to be optimal in that the appropriate weight is given to instability and because workers must self-insure. Any exogenous reduction in the degree of volatility would lead to an expansion of the unstable industry relative to the other sector.

For comparison with the cases described in the following sections, let us suppose that the smoothly distributed annual earnings in the stable industry are $25,000, while the fluctuating earnings in the unstable industry are $26,000. The difference of $1,000 represents the cost of self-insurance.

*Private Unemployment Insurance*

Consider now that there is a private UI program, which can offer a constant annual income stream to workers in the unstable industry at a uniform price per employee that is less than the cost of self-insurance. An insurance company might be able to offer such a relatively cheap contract by pooling the risk of income loss both across individual workers and over time. In practice, the insurance company would have to charge premiums that might be substantial during periods of employment and then return most, but not all, of them as benefits during periods of unemployment. The administrative costs, as well as normal profits for insurance provision, are covered by the difference between total premiums and total benefit payments. Accordingly, we define two income concepts for employees in the unstable industry: *gross* income is the total average annual income received from the employer, while *net* or disposable income is the gross income plus total benefits received minus total premiums paid. Movement by workers between the two industries ensures that the net income in the unstable industry equals the gross income (which is identical to net income) in the stable industry.

In comparison with the case of workers' self-insurance, relative labor costs have fallen in the unstable industry, so that there will be a tendency for it to expand. In other words, since risk pooling through insurance has removed part of the undesirable effects of instability, the activity in the unstable industry is likely to expand at the expense of the other.

The introduction of private insurance has given rise to two possible moral hazard problems. First, since the insurance companies pay the full salary as long as individuals remain unemployed, workers have no incentive to accept any new job if they value the leisure time afforded by being unemployed. This "free rider" situation may be avoided partially by proper policing of the insurance contract or by increasing worker participation in the insurance. Clearly, increases in such participation may be obtained through experience rating of individual workers or through benefit payments that decline with the duration of unemployment.

The second type of moral hazard arises from the behavior of employers. Employers have no incentive to increase the degree of employment smoothing because all employees already enjoy even incomes. Hence, personnel would not be prepared to give up income for employment stability. Some degree of worker participation in the insurance may, again, remove part of this moral hazard.

In terms of the previous numerical example, assume that the private insurance industry can offer insurance at a price of $500 a year. A possible long-run equilibrium may then be established by an annual average (gross and net) income of $25,300 in the stable industry and a gross average income of $25,800 in the unstable industry, of which workers pay $500 to insurance companies and retain $25,300 as net average annual income.

### Public Insurance with a Uniform Tax on Employers

We now assume that, in lieu of the private insurance of the last section, a public UI system is introduced, which is financed by a uniform tax imposed on all employers in both industries. For simplicity, as before, we assume that, due to the UI program, all workers in the unstable industry receive a constant flow of disposable income, including the unemployment benefits when on layoff. Hence, there is no need for self-insurance, and competition equalizes disposable incomes in the two industries.

Suppose that the uniform employer tax is a payroll tax that raises labor costs in both industries by a proportionately equal amount. In comparison with the case of workers' self-insurance, this increase in labor costs is offset to some degree by the disappearance of the risk premium on earnings in the unstable industry, while there is no offset in the other industry. The stable sector is made to bear some of the costs of the fluctuations in the unstable sector. Consequently, the latter expands relative to the former, and the average instability in the economy increases.

Public insurance with a uniform payroll tax may generate the same two moral hazard problems as private insurance. First, there is the possibility that, while unemployed, workers postpone the acceptance of a job offer because their cost of unemployment is very low or zero. Second, employers have no motivation to enhance employment smoothing: they cannot expect to pay lower wages by offering less job volatility, since all workers currently have complete earnings stability. As in the case of private insurance, both types of moral hazard may be partially avoided by raising worker participation in the insurance.

Continuing our numerical illustrations, a new long-run equilibrium might now have the following characteristics. Let the disposable incomes in both industries be $24,000, of which, in the unstable industry, $1,125 consists of UI benefits. There is a 2.4 percent uniform payroll tax, which amounts to $576 per employee in the stable industry and $549 [= 0.024($24,000 - $1,125)] per employee in the unstable industry. Hence, the annual marginal cost of an employee is $24,576 (that is, $24,000 + $576) in the stable industry and $23,424 (that is, $24,000 - $1,125 + $549) in the unstable industry. Any administrative cost of the system would raise the payroll tax, but this would not affect the main arguments concerning the effects of a uniform UI tax. As compared with self-insurance by employees, the relative marginal cost of labor falls in the unstable industry and rises in the stable industry; this tends to lead to an expansion of the unstable industry and a contraction of the stable industry.

### Public Insurance with an Experience-Rated Payroll Tax

We now allow for an experience-rated UI tax. It differs from the uniform tax in that employers' tax rates are linked to the claims experience of their own employees.

A concept that may be useful in the following discussion is the *degree of experience rating*. This measure ranges from *zero* to *full*, and then to *complete*. A zero degree of experience rating corresponds to a uniform tax, which has already been discussed. Complete experience rating is defined as the immediate and total payment by employers of their employees' UI claims.[1] We define an intermediate degree of experience rating as full experience rating. This exists when each employer is assigned a tax rate appropriate to his/her risk class. A specific risk class consists of employers with similar claims experiences, so that their tax liabilities, when averaged over a sufficiently long period of time, are the same. In the short run, any one employer may have a deficit or a surplus with the other members of the risk class, but, in the long run, all employers pay fully for the UI claims of their own employees.

Two important implications of a public UI system with experience rating are worth emphasizing. First, when there is some degree of experience rating, but it is not complete, this type of UI plan provides insurance to employers as well as to employees. Unemployment benefits serve to smooth employees' income streams, and the experience-rated tax structure tends to generate an even tax flow for employers. It thus serves to smooth also the employers' cash flows.

Second, there is no direct link between the degree of experience rating in the employer tax structure and the amount of income smoothing provided to qualified unemployed workers. Complete employee income smoothing may coexist with no experience rating or with complete experience rating. The degree of experience rating affects only the amount and timing of the employer's tax flows. In this respect, an experience-rated public UI system is crucially different from a typical private insurance program. Under private systems, complete experience rating is tantamount to self-insurance by employees, while, under public systems, it leads to self-insurance by employers only, with no impact on employee insurance. Indeed, complete experience rating may be viewed as a mechanism through which employers provide UI to their own employees at the price of reduced average earnings. If employers are less risk averse than employees, such an arrangement is clearly beneficial to both parties.

Consider again our two-industry example, and suppose that the UI tax is fully experience rated so that employers in the unstable industry pay wholly for the cost of the unemployment benefits over an appropriate period of time. Further, in our illustration, employers in the stable industry pay no UI taxes because their employees never draw unemployment benefits. As in the case of the uniform tax previously discussed, employees in the unstable industry are assumed to receive a constant flow of disposable income at the same annual rate as employees in the stable industry.

Thus, employees in the unstable industry, when on layoff, receive their full disposable income in the form of unemployment benefits. There is no need for any residual self-insurance by these employees, and the expected annual disposable incomes are the same in both industries. The employers in this industry must now pay, as part of their labor costs, for the unemployment benefits received by their employees plus any administrative costs of the insurance. Full experience rating ensures that UI does not lead to a significant change in the relative marginal costs of labor in the two industries. As with self-insurance and private insurance, but in contrast to public insurance with a uniform tax, there is no incentive to expand the unstable sector at the expense of the stable sector.

As far as the moral hazard, there is an important difference between, on the one hand, private insurance and public insurance with a uniform tax and, on the other hand, public insurance with an experience-rated tax. This distinction arises from employer incentives to control layoffs. Under an experience-rated tax, employers receive a direct reward, via reduced taxes, for marginally reducing their layoffs. No such direct marginal reward exists under private insurance or public insurance with a uniform tax. Experience rating serves to remove, at least partially, some of the inherent UI inefficiencies due to moral hazard. The other cause of moral hazard, the incentive for the jobless to reject alternative employment offers, remains unaffected.[2]

A numerical example may again be helpful. Suppose that the disposable income in both industries is $25,200. In the stable industry, this consists entirely of earnings, while in the unstable industry, disposable income consists of $22,500 received as earnings from employers plus $2,700 in unemployment benefits. With full experience rating, employers in the unstable industry are subject to an average payroll tax of 12 percent, which is just adequate to raise the $2,700 for the benefits paid to employees. Any costs of administering the system would increase the payroll tax.

### The Case for Experience Rating

A comparison of a public UI system with no experience rating (i.e., a uniform tax) with one that is fully experience rated yields two key conclusions. First, unless all employers in the system belong to the same risk class, a uniform tax will lead to a distortion of relative prices and thus the cross-subsidization of unstable by stable activities. As a result, unstable activities are encouraged, and stable ones are discouraged. Full experience rating avoids these problems and generates an allocation of resources similar to that of well-functioning markets. Less-than-full experience rating leads to cross-subsidization.

Joseph Becker (1972, 1981) emphasized the distortion of relative prices and the consequent cross-subsidization in the UI system when there is less-than-full experience rating. He referred to these problems as inappropriate "cost accounting." Further, his empirical investigations showed that construction firms tended to be heavily subsidized by other businesses, especially those in finance, the services, and trade. In the long run, this situation must be expected to lead to relatively low output prices, relatively high real wages, and relative overproduction in the subsidized sectors as compared to the operation of perfect markets. For further analysis, see Adams (1986).

Subsequent empirical work has confirmed Becker's original research finding of substantial cross-subsidization among firms and industries. The most recent microeconomic empirical analyses of cross-subsidization have been presented in Laurence (1993) and Anderson and Meyer (1994). An attempt at estimating the impact of the cross-subsidization upon relative employment levels was undertaken by Deere (1991), who concluded that "a 10% increase in the implicit subsidy to a layoff increases the employment share in construction by about 1.7% and decreases the employment share in services by almost 1%."

The second basic difference between a uniform and an experience-rated UI tax relates to the incentives for employers to control layoffs by changing employment practices. Many theoretical aspects of the incentive effects of experience rating have been treated in the literature. Two well-known articles are the ones by Feldstein (1976) and Baily (1978). In addition, Brechling (1977) has presented a model of the incentive effects in the institutional framework of the most common U.S. method of experience rating (that is, the reserve ratio method). This line of research has been continued by Wolcowitz (1984) and Cook (1992).

Briefly, the argument states that since experience rating implies a marginal tax cost for layoffs, a cost-minimizing employer will attempt to adjust layoff practices in response to increases in the degree of experience rating, so as to reduce the level of layoffs, benefit payments, and, hence, employer taxes. The incentive is optimized when there is full experience rating because this would lead to the same level of layoffs that would be generated in perfectly working commodity, capital, and labor markets. This result is especially clear in the Feldstein (1976) model.

### The Case against Experience Rating

We are aware of two kinds of counterarguments to the case for experience rating. Since these criticisms have usually been made in comments on papers or in conversation, it is difficult to credit them to particular individuals. Hence, they are presented here without attribution.

1. It is often argued that individual employers do not react to experience rating by altering their layoff patterns. There are two versions of this position. First, the shifting of the tax removes any incentive for firms to control their layoffs, and, second, even with an appropriate incentive, employers are unable to control layoffs. Let us consider these two versions in turn.

The first line of reasoning is that since the burden of the UI tax is likely to be shifted forward via changes in output prices or backward via changes in wages, it cannot have any incentive effects; thus, experience rating cannot be effective in reducing layoffs. This argument is based on the implicit assumption that tax shifting takes place instantaneously, automatically, and at the level of the individual employer. Suppose, for example, that an employer is considering a change in maternity leave policy that, *ceteris paribus*, would reduce taxes by $X$ and have a marginal cost of $Y$. If the employer would invariably have to pass on the entire net marginal surplus of $(X - Y)$ to workers in the form of increased wages (and/or to customers in the form of reduced output prices), then the marginal return to the employer would always be zero. Here, tax shifting has been defined in such a narrow fashion that the employer has no inducement to introduce new technology, because any net benefit in the form of higher profits is immediately passed on to others. Thus, there cannot be a profit motive, as economists normally understand that concept.

This narrow view of tax shifting is not supported in the relevant public finance literature. The approach is also incompatible with competitive theory in which prices and wages are determined by market demand and supply and cannot be influenced by the actions of an individual employer.

In contrast to the narrow view of tax shifting, it seems reasonable to assume, as we have done in the illustrative two-industry model, that some industry average of the UI tax is shifted forward or backward and that the behavior of any one employer does not affect the average tax significantly. In this case, individual employers correctly treat their output prices and wages (or compensation packages) as independent of their own attempts to reduce their tax bills; employers can reap, through higher profits, the full net benefits of any changes in layoff patterns that accrue to them through experience rating.

The second version of the argument is based on the assumption that, because employers cannot change their layoff and employment patterns, they have very limited ability to respond to the incentives of experience rating. Hence, experience rating may be unfair for employers who operate in markets with particularly uncertain and volatile conditions.

In our view, the level of incentives of the tax system and degree to which employers can and do respond to these incentives must be determined primarily by empirical investigation, not by theoretical argument. In a very general empirical framework, it is well known that Japanese employment practices lead to substantially lower layoff rates (and unemployment levels) than are customary in the U.S., yet Japanese firms have been well able to compete successfully in international markets. Hence, it would appear that there are some opportunities for U.S. employers to change their layoff patterns. Furthermore, empirical work in the U.S. institutional framework has shown repeatedly that employers do react to high marginal tax costs of layoffs by reducing layoffs. The initial findings by Feldstein (1978), Brechling (1981), Clark and Summers (1982), and Topel (1983) have been supplemented recently by the research of Card and Levine (1994) and Anderson and

Meyer (1994). We, therefore, reject the assertion that, in general, employers cannot control their layoff patterns under an experience-rated UI tax structure.

2. It is sometimes argued that experience rating violates the basic principles of insurance and that it should be incomplete or even be replaced by a uniform tax. Our discussion earlier in this section has shown that full experience rating is quite compatible with accepted insurance principles. With experience rating, both employers and employees can be provided with some insurance. Even if experience rating were complete, only employers would lose their coverage, while employees would remain insured.

## The Two Dominant Methods of Experience Rating

The UI system in the U.S. has been established under both federal and state laws. The federal statutes lay down general guidelines, under which the states have substantial leeway to fashion systems to suit their own circumstances. Thus, the Federal Unemployment Tax Act (FUTA) mandates that there be experience-rated payroll taxes, but the determination of the exact method of experience rating is left to the individual states. States have enacted various methods of experience rating and, within the same methods, different parameter values. Two forms of experience rating are used predominantly:[3] the reserve ratio method (used in 32 states) and the benefit ratio method (used in 15 states). Although these approaches have much in common, their differences may have important implications for the economic incentives they give to employers to alter employment patterns. First, we will review the common characteristics of these approaches.

### *Common Features of the Two Experience-Rating Methods*

The two experience-rating methods share five features. These elements are (1) the computation of the taxable payroll, (2) the concept of charged benefits, (3) time lags, (4) the suspension of experience rating under certain circumstances, and (5) trust fund solvency provisions.

## The Taxable Payroll

The firm's UI *tax bill* ($T$) for a particular calendar year is the product of its *tax rate* ($\tau$) and its *taxable payroll* ($W$) for that year. The taxable payroll, in turn, consists of the cumulated earnings of all employees up to the *taxable wage base* ($\hat{w}$) for each employee in each calendar year. On January 1, the process of cumulating earnings starts over again. The minimum taxable wage base is set by FUTA, but higher bases may be mandated by state legislatures. In 1994, the federal taxable wage base was $7,000 and the state bases ranged up to $25,000.

Throughout this book, we assume that the taxable payroll per employee is equal to the taxable wage base and that the employer's total taxable payroll is the product of the taxable wage base and the mean of the employment levels at the beginning and the end of the year.

Thus, if the taxable wage base is $10,000 and the employer's workforce falls from 500 at the beginning of the calendar year to 400 at the end of the year, the taxable payroll is assumed to be ($10,000) (1/2) (500 + 400) = $4,500,000.

The preceding approximation of the taxable payroll may be distorted for two reasons. First, employment growth may not be smooth between January 1 and December 31, so that the average employment in the example may not be 450. Second, even if the level of employment does not change during the year, interfirm labor turnover tends to influence the size of the taxable payroll. Suppose, for example, that the taxable wage base is $10,000 and that the annual wage paid in a particular job is $20,000. If the job is filled by one employee for the entire year, then the taxable payroll with respect to this position is $10,000. If, on the other hand, the same job is filled by one employee in the first six months and by a different employee during the second six months, then the taxable payroll is $20,000 because the employer has to cumulate earnings up to $10,000 for each employee. See Brechling (1977) for a general formulation and elaboration of these points and Brechling (1981) for an empirical verification.

Our approximation of the taxable payroll may be stated in equation form:

$$(2.1) \quad W_t = \hat{w}\frac{1}{2}(N_t + N_{t-1}),$$

where $N_t$ represents employment at year-end and $N_{t-1}$ represents employment at the beginning of year $t$. In general, the subscript $t$ refers to a calendar year. The equation relates to the formal analysis that will be developed in later chapters.

### Charged Benefits

An employer's unemployment experience is measured by his/her *charged benefits* (*CB*) under both the reserve and the benefit ratio methods of experience rating. Charged benefits are the total annual unemployment benefits that have been paid to the employer's laid-off workers and that have been deemed to be chargeable to the employer's account. Not all unemployment benefits are chargeable. Examples of *noncharged benefits* are benefits paid to voluntary quitters, some "extended" benefits legislated specifically in particularly severe recessions, and some benefits paid for employee dependents.

Charged benefits arise from both temporary and permanent layoffs. Temporary layoffs are those leading only to relatively short-lived reductions in employment. These cutbacks are reversed by new hires or recalls after fairly brief periods of time. From the perspective of our current discussion, as introduced in chapter 1, the most important characteristic of temporary layoffs is that they do not lead to significant long-run reductions in the taxable payroll. Permanent layoffs, by contrast, are defined as lasting curtailments in the work force and do imply a decrease in the taxable payroll.

It should perhaps be pointed out that the distinction between temporary and permanent layoffs need not necessarily correspond to the unemployment experiences of individual workers. As an example, suppose that worker A is laid off and that worker B is hired as a replacement after a short time. If A remains unemployed for a long period, then the layoff is regarded as temporary by the employer but as permanent by the employee. In this study, layoffs are categorized as temporary or permanent according to the employer's perception. To be sure, since the rate of recall is typically very high among temporary layoffs, the latter are likely to be perceived as temporary by both the employer and by most of the affected employees.

Our subsequent analysis is facilitated by specifying a *temporary layoff rate* (*u*), which measures the proportion of the average stock of employees laid off in a calendar year. Thus, if the layoff rate is 10 percent and the average level of employment is 450 (as in the preceding example), then the hypothetical employer effects 45 temporary layoffs in the calendar year. Permanent layoffs are measured by the net reduction in the level of employment over the course of the calendar year. In the example, permanent layoffs amount to 100 (i.e., 500 − 400). Permanent layoffs are zero when the employer adds to employment over the course of the year.

Both temporary and permanent layoffs qualify for unemployment benefits. The weekly benefit payment ($\hat{b}$) is determined by state law, usually at about one-half of previous earnings, subject to a maximum. We shall use the concept of *benefits per unemployment spell* (*b*). This is simply the product of the weekly benefit payment and the number of weeks that the laid-off worker receives unemployment compensation. Thus, if the weekly benefit payment is $250 and the duration of the unemployment spell is 12 weeks, the benefit per unemployment spell is (12) ($250) = $3,000. This would be the amount of benefits charged to the employer's account with respect to each layoff. In practice, the weekly benefit payment and the unemployment duration are likely to differ among employees. Hence, the $3,000 should be considered as an average for all layoffs.

The level of charged benefits can be expressed as the following equation:

$$(2.2) \quad CB_t = b \left[ u_t \frac{1}{2} (N_{t-1} + N_t) + (N_{t-1} - N_t) \right]$$

where   $(N_{t-1} - N_t) = (N_{t-1} - N_t)$ if $(N_{t-1} - N_t) > 0$
and     $(N_{t-1} - N_t) = 0$ if $(N_{t-1} - N_t) \leq 0$.

The first term in the square brackets in equation (2.2) represents temporary layoffs, and the second term represents permanent layoffs.

*Time Lags*

With both types of experience rating, there are substantial periods of time between the year when unemployment benefits are paid and charged to an employer and the year when the tax rate changes. Typically, the employer tax rate for 1994, for example, would have been determined between June and October of 1993, based on the layoff experience over the years 1990, 1991, and 1992. These time lags prevent the immediate response of taxes to charged benefits and may cause inequality between a firm's charged benefits and its tax payments in any particular year. Furthermore, neither method allows for interest payments or discounting. Thus, even if the firm pays $100 in taxes for each $100 of charged benefits, the lag of the former behind the latter implies that, *in present value terms*, tax payments fall short of charged benefits.

### Suspension of Experience Rating

Experience rating is partially or fully suspended in certain circumstances under both the reserve ratio and the benefit ratio methods. In particular, minimum and maximum tax rates ($\tau_{MIN}$ and $\tau_{MAX}$) are specified by state laws. Changes in charged benefits do not affect these minimum or maximum tax rates, and, as long as an employer is and expects to remain at the minimum or maximum tax rate, changes in charged benefits cannot affect his/her tax bill. The minimum tax rate ensures that all employers make a minimal contribution to the UI system. It is usually regarded as necessary to pay for the noncharged benefits that are not attributable to any particular employer. The maximum rate alleviates the tax burden for employers with particularly high past unemployment experiences. At the maximum and minimum rates, benefits are said to be *ineffectively* charged because they are not allowed to influence employers' individual tax rates.

Experience rating is also absent for new employers since they have no history of layoffs. Typically, they are assigned an initial fixed tax rate until they acquire the necessary unemployment experience.[4] In some states, this tax rate varies according to the unemployment experience of the industry in which the new employer is located.

Another suspension of experience rating occurs in the case of bankrupt or inactive employers. The costs of unemployment benefits paid to these employers' laid-off workers may be charged to the employers' accounts, but since they have ceased to operate, their payrolls and tax liabilities are zero, no matter what their accumulated charged benefits may be.

### Trust Fund Solvency

If all unemployment benefits were fully charged and there were no time lags or suspensions in the experience-rating methods, the current tax payments of all employers would be adequate to pay for all current unemployment benefits. If, in addition, a small tax were levied to recover administration costs, then the UI system would be totally self-financed in any particular year. Since the required conditions are not satisfied, however, the UI system may run an annual deficit or surplus. To allow for the carry-over of deficit or surplus balances from one year to another, state trust funds have been established. Employer tax payments (as well as interest and some other disbursements from the federal government) are credited to the state's trust fund, and unemployment benefit payments are debited.

To ensure the long-run solvency of their trust funds, all states have made provisions for some or all tax rates to rise (fall) as the trust fund balance, expressed as a percentage of the state's total taxable payroll, falls (rises).[5] These changes in tax schedules are automatic and do not require specific legislation. States differ in the methods by which their tax structures respond to changes in the trust fund balance. In Louisiana, for example, a falling trust fund balance triggers equiproportionate increases in experience-rated tax rates. Thus, with given taxable payrolls, employers with high UI tax rates face larger increases in their tax bills than do employers with low tax rates. In Mississippi, by contrast, a fixed absolute amount is added to all UI tax rates, thus distributing the tax burden equally across employers. As a third illustration, Minnesota raises just the minimum tax rate ($\tau_{MIN}$), thus only raising the tax burden of employers with the best experience record. Though the distribution of the extra tax burden may differ among states, all states have made provisions for aggregate tax inflows to increase as the trust fund declines or, indeed, becomes negative.

In general, state laws governing employer experience rating may be regarded as allocating UI costs to individual employers. Laws governing changes in average tax rates are designed to ensure the solvency of the system as a whole.

While the reserve ratio and the benefit ratio methods of experience rating may be viewed from the perspective of their common dimensions, these two approaches differ in several important respects. We now turn to a description of their unique characteristics.

### Distinctive Features of the Two Experience-Rating Methods

#### The Reserve Ratio Method

Under the reserve ratio method of experience rating, each employer is assigned an account similar to an ordinary checking account. The account contains the employer's past tax payments as deposits and past charged benefits as debits. During any particular year, the balance in this account rises by the amount of tax payments and falls by the amount of charged benefits. At the end of a year $t$, the balance $(B_t)$, which may be negative, is thus equal to all past tax payments minus all past charged benefits. As noted before, according to current laws, the employer neither receives interest on positive balances nor pays interest on negative balances.

The employer's reserve ratio ($RR$) is defined as the ratio of the balance to the taxable payroll, where the latter is usually averaged over the past three-to-five calendar years. The reserve ratio is usually expressed as a percentage. As an example, assume that the hypothetical employer had the following taxable payrolls:

$$1990 — \$4,500,000$$
$$1991 — \$4,700,000$$
$$1992 — \$4,800,000$$

With a balance at the end of 1992 of \$200,000, the employer's reserve ratio at the end of 1992 would have been:

$$RR_{92} = 100\left[\frac{200,000}{\left(\frac{1}{3}\right)(4,500,000 + 4,700,000 + 4,800,000)}\right]$$

$$= 100(.0429) = 4.29\%.$$

The essence of the reserve ratio method of experience rating is the negative link between the reserve ratio and the tax rate. Figure 2.1 illustrates a typical tax schedule.[6] The tax rate for year $t$ is measured along the vertical axis, and the lagged reserve ratio is shown along the horizontal axis. The schedule is kinked at $\underline{RR}$ below which $\tau_{MAX}$ applies, and at $\overline{RR}$ above which $\tau_{MIN}$ applies. As previously mentioned, the tax rate responds to changes in the reserve ratio with a substantial lag. Typically, the firm's tax rate for year $t$ is determined in the June-October period of year $(t-1)$ on the basis of the firm's reserve ratio at the end of year $(t-2)$.[7] The tax schedule in figure 2.1 is valid only for a particular range of values of the state trust fund balance. Higher schedules apply for lower trust fund balances (expressed as a percentage of the statewide taxable payroll), and vice versa. In the tax codes of reserve ratio states, the various schedules are usually presented in tabular form.

**Figure 2.1   Reserve Ratio Tax Schedule**

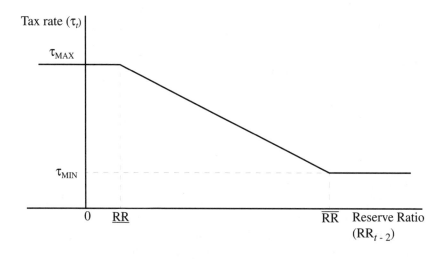

The reserve ratio (4.29 percent for the end of 1992—or later in some states) can be located on the horizontal axis in figure 2.1. The corresponding tax rate (for 1994, in the example) can then be read off the vertical axis.

We now state the main characteristics of the reserve ratio method in formal terms. The employer's balance $B$ at the end of year $t$ is defined as:

$$(2.3) \quad B_t = B_{t-1} + T_t - CB_t = \sum_{i=0}^{m} (T_{t-i} - CB_{t-i}),$$

where $m$ is the total number of years for which the employer has had an account and $i$ is a counter from 0 to $m$. As before, the time subscript $t$ dates stocks (such as the balance $B$) at the end of the year and flows (such as tax payments $T$) during the year. The reserve ratio $RR$ is defined as the ratio of the firm's balance to a moving average of its taxable payroll $W$:

$$(2.4) \quad RR_t = (n+1) \frac{B_t}{\displaystyle\sum_{i=0}^{n} W_{t-i}},$$

where $(n+1)$ is the number of years over which the moving average of the taxable payroll is calculated. Typically $(n+1)$ is three-to-five years.

As discussed, the essential element of the reserve ratio method of experience rating is that the tax rate $\tau$ and the reserve ratio $RR$ are negatively related:

$$(2.5) \quad \tau_t = a - s\,(\chi_{1t}\underline{RR} + \chi_{2t}RR_{t-2} + \chi_{3t}\overline{RR}),$$

where $a$ is the intercept of the tax schedule, which must be positive, and $s$ is the slope of the tax schedule, which should lie between 0 and 1. Typically, $a$ is in the range of 5 to 8 percent and $s$ is in the range of 0.25 to 0.50. As previously mentioned, there are minimum and maximum tax rates ($\tau_{\mathrm{MAX}}$ and $\tau_{\mathrm{MIN}}$) that are triggered at critically low $(\underline{RR})$ and high $(\overline{RR})$ reserve ratios. The $\chi$s are dummy variables that represent the three ranges of the tax schedule. Specifically,

1. When $RR_{t-2} \le \underline{RR}$ then $(\chi_{1t}, \chi_{2t}, \chi_{3t}) = (1, 0, 0)$
   and $\tau_t = \tau_{\mathrm{MAX}} = a - s\underline{RR}$; the firm is at the maximum tax rate.

2. When $\underline{RR} < RR_{t-2} < \overline{RR}$ then $(\chi_{1t}, \chi_{2t}, \chi_{3t}) = (0, 1, 0)$
   and $\tau_t = \tau_{\mathrm{SLOPE}} = a - sRR_{t-2}$; the firm is on the experience-rated segment of the tax schedule.

3. When $\overline{RR} \le RR_{t-2}$ then $(\chi_{1t}, \chi_{2t}, \chi_{3t}) = (0, 0, 1)$
   and $\tau_t = \tau_{\mathrm{MIN}} = a - s\overline{RR}$; the firm is at the minimum tax rate.

*The Benefit Ratio Method*

Under the benefit ratio method of experience rating, the firm's tax rate is related positively to its benefit ratio *BR*. The benefit ratio is defined as the ratio of a moving average of charged benefits $CB_t$ to a moving average of the taxable payroll $W_t$. Usually the averages are computed over three to five calendar years. Thus, in the example of the previous section, the hypothetical employer's average taxable payroll for the years 1990, 1991, and 1992 was $4,666,667. With an average annual level of charged benefits of $140,000 over the same three years, the benefit ratio for this period would be 140,000/4,666,667 = 3 percent. For the sake of brevity, we shall refer to it as the 1992 benefit ratio ($BR_{92}$).

The benefit ratio method of experience rating is based on a positive relationship between the tax rate in year *t*, which is 1994, in the present example, and the benefit ratio in year ($t - 2$), which is 1992 in the present example. The tax schedule is illustrated in figure 2.2. It shows that $\tau_{MIN}$ applies when the benefit ratio is below $\underline{BR}$, varies positively with the benefit ratio along the sloped part of the schedule, and is fixed at $\tau_{MAX}$ when the benefit ratio is above $\overline{BR}$. As in the case of the reserve ratio method, the tax schedule in figure 2.2 moves up and down automatically when the state's trust fund balance (as a percentage of the statewide taxable payroll) falls or rises. Given a 1992 benefit ratio, the corresponding tax rate for 1994 can be read from the vertical axis of the figure.

More formally, the benefit ratio for an employer is defined as

$$(2.6) \quad BR_t = \frac{\sum_{i=0}^{n} CB_{t-i}}{\sum_{i=0}^{n} W_{t-i}},$$

where, similar to the case of the reserve ratio method ($n+1$) is the number of calendar years, over which *CB* and *W* are averaged. The complete tax schedule can be expressed as

$$(2.7) \quad \tau_t = c + k\left(\chi_{1t}\underline{BR} + \chi_{2t}BR_{t-2} + \chi_{3t}(\overline{BR})\right),$$

where $c$ is the intercept and $k$ is the slope of the tax schedule. In practice, $c$ and $k$ are often close to zero and unity, respectively. The vector of dummy variables $(\chi_{1t}, \chi_{2t}, X\chi_{3t})$ ensures that the tax schedule consists of three segments, with the following values:

1. When $BR_{t-2} \leq \underline{BR}$, then $(\chi_{1t}, \chi_{2t}, \chi_{3t}) = (1, 0, 0)$
   and $\tau_t = \tau_{MIN} = c + k\underline{BR}$; the firm is at the minimum tax rate.

2. When $\underline{BR} < BR_{t-2} < \overline{BR}$, then $(\chi_{1t}, \chi_{2t}, \chi_{3t}) = (0, 1, 0)$
   and $\tau_t = \tau_{SLOPE} = c + kBR_{t-2}$; the firm is on the experience-rated segment of the tax schedule.

3. When $\overline{BR} \leq BR_{t-2}$, then $(\chi_{1t}, \chi_{2t}, \chi_{3t}) = (0, 0, 1)$
   and $\tau_t = \tau_{MAX} = c + k\overline{BR}_t$; the firm is at the maximum tax rate.

**Figure 2.2   Benefit Ratio Tax Schedule**

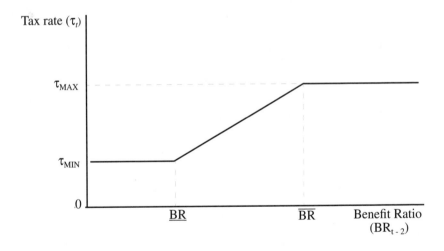

*Basic Differences of the Two Methods*

In evaluating the essential differences between the reserve and benefit ratio methods of experience rating, we first consider the information contained in these measures. The reserve ratio is a summary record of all the employer's past tax payments and charged benefits. It is a comprehensive indicator of the relevant relationships with the UI system.

By contrast, the benefit ratio measures only the charged benefits over the $(n + 1)$ years. Under the reserve ratio method, employers' tax rates are determined by their entire tax and benefit history; under the benefit ratio method, the tax is simply the delayed payment for charged benefits.

Second, since the reserve ratio is a summary of all past benefit and tax payments, this method has a very long memory. With typical parameters, benefits charged 15 years ago may have an influence on the current tax rate. The benefit ratio method, on the other hand, forgets any benefits that were charged prior to $(n + 3)$, for example, five years ago. This point is particularly relevant in a recession, when employers are pushed temporarily to the maximum tax rate, where experience rating is suspended and further benefits are said to be charged ineffectively. Under the benefit ratio method, part or all of these charged benefits will be forgotten; under the reserve ratio method, these benefits will be remembered through the falling reserve ratio, which will cause increased taxes when economic circumstances improve. In other words, benefits are likely to be ineffectively charged permanently under the benefit ratio method and ineffectively charged temporarily under the reserve ratio method.

Third, the reserve ratio method incorporates the concept of a precautionary financial balance, which can be used for temporary deficits. In the course of a typical business cycle, the employer's fund is built up in economic good times and drawn down in bad times. The employer's cyclically fluctuating benefit flow is matched by a fairly smooth tax flow; as a result, the employer has a surplus with the system in booms and a deficit in recessions. The design provides insurance to the employer in accordance with principles described earlier in this chapter. In the absence of business cycles, i.e., when benefit flows are smooth, the reserve ratio method generates a long-run (steady-state) balance and reserve ratio. By contrast, the benefit ratio method is simply a "pay-as-you-go" system, in which payment occurs with a lag. It does not incorporate explicitly the concept of a precautionary balance that can support temporary deficits.

Fourth, the relationship between charged benefits and taxes is more complex and has longer lags under the reserve than under the benefit ratio method. As an illustration, suppose that the tax rate remains at less than the maximum. Under the reserve ratio method, an increase in charged benefits of $100 will reduce, *ceteris paribus*, the balance by $100. This reduction, in turn, will raise taxes after two years by less than $100 (with typical parameter values) but maintain increased taxes for many years until the entire $100 is paid. Under the benefit ratio method, the $100 in benefits would be paid by increased taxes in years 3, 4, and 5.

### The Degree of Experience Rating

We have defined the degree of experience rating in terms of the closeness of the link between charged benefits and the resulting taxes. We will now develop this concept further by specific reference to the two methods of experience rating.

A zero degree of experience rating is achieved under either method when the payroll tax is independent of charged benefits. This would be reflected by a zero slope of the tax schedules in figures 2.1 and 2.2.

The degree of experience rating incorporated in the system would increase as a result of the following parameter changes. First, if the maximum tax rate $\tau_{MAX}$ is raised and/or the minimum tax rate $\tau_{MIN}$ is lowered, then the ranges over which the reserve and benefit ratios are on the sloped parts of the tax schedule increase; thus, the employer is more likely to be experience rated.

Second, the closer the slope of the tax schedule is to unity, the closer is the numerical response of the tax to charged benefits. Therefore, the degree of experience rating is higher.

Third, the shorter the time period between the disbursement of benefits and the payment of taxes, the fewer interest-free loans are made. Consequently, the degree of experience rating is greater.

Fourth, given that there are some irreducible time lags between benefit disbursements, the degree of experience rating can also be raised by appropriate interest charges and credits, so that interest-free loans are precluded. This could be done very easily under the reserve ratio method by paying interest on positive employer fund balances and by charging interest on negative balances.

## Experience Rating and Temporary Layoffs

The relationship between temporary layoffs and an experience-rated UI tax was examined in the previously mentioned papers by Feldstein (1976) and Baily (1977). Their characterization of experience rating was very general, however. As an example, Feldstein simply used the parameter $e$ (which ranges from zero to one) to describe the degree of experience rating. Brechling (1977) used a model of the reserve ratio method of experience rating (without maximum and minimum tax rates) and studied the impact on the incentive to lay off workers. Wolcowitz (1984) extended this work by allowing for maximum and minimum tax rates and by elaborating on the full, dynamic implications of the reserve ratio method. Cook (1992) furthered the analysis by considering the benefit ratio as well as the reserve ratio method of experience rating.

The cited literature is based on a model of the individual firm. The firm can vary temporary layoffs from which it derives some net marginal benefit. In the absence of an experience-rated UI system, optimal layoffs are determined at the point where their net marginal benefits are zero. A constant payroll tax indicates a zero marginal tax cost of layoffs and consequently a relatively high level of layoffs. In contrast, both methods of experience rating may imply positive marginal tax costs of layoffs, thereby giving incentives to employers to reduce layoffs below the level generated by zero net marginal benefits.

In her detailed analysis of the two methods of experience rating, Cook (1992) reaches the following general conclusions. First, the reserve ratio and benefit ratio methods are quite different in their dynamic implications. The reserve ratio method gives rise to dynamic decision rules, which require that the firm adopt optimal *paths* of layoffs crucially dependent on the initial and final reserve ratios. Changes in exogenous factors tend to affect the entire optimal path of layoffs. By contrast, the benefit ratio method results in static decision rules, which require, with unchanged exogenous factors, a constant optimal layoff rate, independent of its future or past levels. Changes in exogenous factors lead to *instantaneous* adjustment in the optimal layoff rate.

Second, when a typical firm starts and expects to remain on the horizontal sections of the tax schedules, that is, at $\tau_{MAX}$ or $\tau_{MIN}$, then, under both methods of experience rating, the marginal tax cost of layoffs is zero, and the layoff rate is the same as under a tax not based on experience rating. In these cases, there is no difference between the two methods of experience rating because neither is operative.

Third, when a hypothetical firm is and expects to remain on the sloped segment of the tax schedule, then both methods of experience rating yield positive marginal tax costs of layoffs and lead to optimal layoffs below those generated by a system without experience rating. Further, the higher the slope of the tax schedule ($s$ or $k$) and the lower the rate of discount (that is, the interest rate), the higher the marginal tax costs will be and the lower the optimal layoff rate. With realistic parameter settings, the implied marginal tax costs are quite similar under the two methods of experience rating. There are no *inherent* characteristics of the two methods that give rise to differences in layoff behavior when the firm starts and remains on the slope of the tax schedule.

Fourth, when, due to some exogenous change, the firm starts on one segment of the tax schedule and ends up on another, the two methods lead to different behavior. The reserve ratio method adjusts layoffs gradually from the old to the new level, while the benefit ratio adjusts layoffs instantaneously to the new equilibrium level. Thus, when the firm moves from the sloped to the flat segments of the tax schedule, the reserve ratio method leads to lower average layoff rates than the benefit ratio method. On the other hand, when the firm moves from the flat to the sloped segments of the tax schedules, the benefit ratio method leads to lower average layoff rates than the reserve ratio method.

As previously discussed, the results of empirical work over the past 15 years or so seem to lend substantial support to the theoretical claim that the degree of experience rating has a significant negative impact on the level of temporary layoffs and on unemployment. In the work by Topel (1983), Card and Levine (1994), and Anderson and Meyer (1994), the characteristics of the two experience-rating methods are embodied in the estimates of the "marginal tax costs" (MTC) of layoffs. Hence, any essential differences between the two methods of experience rating should be reflected in differences in their MTCs.

## Concluding Remarks

We have attempted to set the stage for the analysis to be presented in the following chapters. The primary concern of previous investigators of experience rating has been its impact on temporary layoffs. Unemployment benefits for temporary layoffs are often justified in terms of insurance principles. Insurance serves to maintain disposable incomes of employees during temporary layoffs, and employees pay for this service via reduced average earnings.

In the U.S. system, employers are directly responsible for the payment of UI taxes. This gives rise to a possible additional insurance attribute, the smoothing of the typical employer's cash flows.

In customary private insurance arrangements (e.g., automobile insurance), experience rating is applied to the premiums paid by the insurant. Experience rating in public UI situations, on the other hand, refers to the experience of employers. When experience rating is full, employers pay, over an appropriately long period of time, for all the unemployment benefits received by their own former workers. When experience rating is less than full, there exists (1) long-run cross-subsidization of one group of firms by another, which, in turn, leads to a misallocation of resources, and (2) a possibly substantial moral hazard problem, which implies nonoptimally large layoffs. When experience rating is complete, employers pay fully and immediately for all of their former employees' benefits. Thus, employers lose their (cash flow smoothing) insurance entirely, but employees are still insured.

Empirical investigations of UI taxes and benefits have shown that there are sizable cross-subsidizations, so that, by and large, actual experience-rating systems in the U.S. are less than full. Further, there is now convincing evidence that increases in the degree of experience rating reduce layoffs significantly. For these reasons, an increase in the degree of UI experience rating for temporary layoffs is a desirable social goal.

We have described the technical aspects of the two most common experience-rated UI tax systems as well as their implications for temporary layoffs. The methods differ in their dynamic effects and in the length of their memory. The degree of experience rating can be elevated by (1) raising the maximum tax rate, (2) lowering the minimum tax rate, (3) increasing the slope of the tax schedule, if it is below unity, or (4) charging interest on outstanding benefits. We have a preference for the reserve ratio method of experience rating because it has a longer memory and can easily be amended to reflect the appropriate financial cost—by paying interest on employers' positive balances and by charging interest on negative balances.

Against this background, we now turn to an examination of permanent layoffs. Three basic questions will be addressed. How important are permanent as compared to temporary layoffs? How should the costs of permanent layoffs be covered? How do the two most common methods of experience rating treat the costs of permanent layoffs?

## NOTES

1. Complete experience rating is actually approximated in the U.S. by the so-called reimbursable method of experience rating, for which certain not-for-profit companies and local government agencies qualify. See also note 3.

2. In the preceding discussion, we have assumed, for the sake of expository ease, that workers receive unemployment benefits equal to their previous earnings, that is, that the replacement ratio is unity. In practice, replacement ratios are 40 to 60 percent; thus, there is a substantial amount of self-insurance by employees. The more self-insurance there is, the less important are the moral hazard problems associated with the three types of insurance systems.

3. The other two types of experience rating are the benefit wage ratio method, used in two states, and the payroll decline method, used in one state. In addition, there is the reimbursable method (mentioned in note 1), which may be chosen by qualifying nonprofit and government employers in all states. The reimbursable method is not related to a payroll tax. Employers are simply sent a bill for UI benefits paid to their employees.

4. The time period over which a new firm pays a tax not based on experience rating ranges from one to four years.

5. Negative trust fund balances imply that the states must borrow from the federal government. States have to pay interest on these loans. Furthermore, the Secretary of Labor may impose a special federal tax to recoup loans to state trust funds. Thus, states have definite incentives to avoid negative trust fund balances.

6. Most actual tax schedules consist of small steps along the sloped part and of one or two larger steps in the neighborhood of the zero reserve ratio.

7. In figure 2.1, the reserve ratio at the end of 1992 determines the tax rate in 1994. Some states use a shorter lag between the reserve ratio and the tax rate. For instance, in New York State, the reserve ratio for December 31, 1993, is computed as the ratio of the firm's trust fund balance on that date to the taxable payroll for the period of October 1, 1992 to September 30, 1993. The tax rate for 1994 is then determined on the basis of the reserve ratio on December 31, 1993. The longer lag, presented in the text, is used by most states.

# 3
# Recent Trends in Permanent and Temporary Layoffs

How important are temporary layoffs in comparison to permanent layoffs? If declines in employment are for the most part temporary, then the design of the unemployment insurance (UI) system should be such that the firm creating the layoff pays for the benefits received by workers. However, if much of the employment decline is permanent, this pool of unemployed labor serves as a reserve available for growing firms to hire (Hall 1971). The expanding enterprise gains from the permanent layoff and thus may be assessed part of the associated UI cost.

Using unpublished data from the National Longitudinal Survey (1966-1971) of work experience of men between the ages of 45 and 59, Feldstein (1976) found that 61 percent of the unemployed were on temporary layoff. Crosslin, Hanna, and Stevens, who used data from the ES-202 Report and from the U.S. Department of Labor's Continuous Wage and Benefit History program data base (1979-1983) for five states, concurred with Feldstein's results. Yet, Murphy and Topel (1987), working with information from the Annual Demographic File (1968-1985) of the Current Population Survey (CPS), found that, for males between the ages of 18 and 64, permanent, not temporary, separations accounted for a larger fraction of the unemployment rate. This relationship persisted over the study period as unemployment rose in the downturn of the business cycle, except during 1975, when temporary, rather than permanent, layoffs were a higher fraction of the unemployment rate.

Using firm and individual employment information from the UI administrative records of six states, Anderson and Meyer (1994) decomposed the fraction of employees receiving benefits into those on temporary or on permanent layoff. They found that the proportion of employees receiving UI benefits on permanent layoff ranged from 24 to 66 percent across the six states.

## The Data

Our study utilizes two longitudinal data sets for establishments from the records of the Texas Employment Commission, which administers the UI program in the state. The first set contains quarterly employment statistics for 101,169 establishments, either with continuous employment or declared bankruptcy, from the years 1978 to 1982. This sample represents 60 percent of employment in the state.[1] The second set comprises monthly employment data for 822,713 establishments from 1978 to 1989. The establishments constitute all those in the state with covered employment during the period. However, a maximum of approximately 400,000 establishments were in operation in any quarter, such that a large number of births and deaths of establishments occurred over this time span.

Each data set provides a different perspective on the issue of employment reductions. The major strength of both sets is that they enable the calculation of quarter-to-quarter (or month-to-month) employment declines, unlike other sources that may have only annual or decennial data.

Are employment reductions a fair indication of temporary or permanent layoffs? An employment reduction can occur due to one of four reasons: a temporary layoff, a permanent layoff, a quit, or a retirement. A quit or retirement can affect the number of both temporary and permanent employment declines. If an employer maintains a job, then the worker who quits or retires will be replaced. When the replacement occurs prior to the worker's departure, the calculation of respective employment declines is unaffected. Otherwise, the quit or retirement could be counted as either a temporary or a permanent employment decline, depending on how long the position remains vacant. If the employer cuts the number of job positions, then the quit or retirement will be counted as a permanent employment decline.

The importance of retirements in the calculation is difficult to discern. However, Murphy and Topel (1987) indicate that quits represented 10 percent, on average, of the unemployment rate caused by temporary layoffs, separations, and quits from 1968 to 1985. Hence, employer-initiated spells are dominant in unemployment. As previously stated, the proportion of permanent, as opposed to temporary, layoffs during the period is consistently greater, except in 1975.[2]

If quits were equally distributed between temporary and permanent employment declines, the percentage calculation of employment declines representing temporary and permanent layoffs would be unaffected. If quits were associated only with permanent declines, then permanent layoffs would be overestimated by approximately 5 percent.[3] The overrepresentation of permanent layoffs would therefore range between 0 and 5 percent in the calculations presented subsequently in this chapter. How else might these measures be imperfect?

- All reductions in employment may not result in UI benefit payments, although certainly a proportion of these cutbacks would be eligible.

- If the individual is replaced within the time period over which the employment reduction is assessed, then temporary reductions in employment would tend to overestimate temporary layoffs.

- The establishment record does not identify an employment change caused by the sale of only part of the establishment. The employment decline within the establishment would be counted as a permanent decline, such that the calculation of permanent reductions would be overestimated.

- It is not possible to assess whether employment from one quarter to the next (or from one month to the next) represents the same jobs for the same employees. If this is not the case, permanent declines in employment would yield an underestimate of permanent layoffs because some individuals would remain jobless although their former positions had been filled.

## Measurement of Employment Declines

For the measurement of employment declines, we focus on a relatively narrow definition of temporary layoffs. In the macroeconomic literature, in contrast, temporary layoffs may involve longer periods, such as a full business cycle. Our approach considers the fact that UI creates a special relationship between workers and firms, one that can be temporarily broken for up to 26 weeks. For longer layoffs, however, the relationship may be permanently severed as workers have no incentive to wait for recall.[4] Note that 26 weeks is the typical time period for which a worker can collect UI benefits and that the average unemployment spell currently lasts about 15 weeks.

Figures 3.1, 3.2, and 3.3 represent the possible pattern of employment changes for those firms with reductions in employment.[5] To estimate the amount of permanent and temporary employment reductions, the comparisons use A, B, and C as three consecutive points in time. If employment in period B is less than employment in period A, then period C is used as a reference point to determine the status of the employment decline as permanent or temporary. The following algorithm was used:

1. Figure 3.1:
   If employment at C is less than or equal to employment at B, then the change in employment from A to B is permanent.

2. Figure 3.2:
   If employment at C is greater than that at B, but less than that at A, then the change from A to C is permanent and from C to B is temporary.

3. Figure 3.3:
   If employment at C is greater than or equal to employment at A, then the change from A to B is temporary.

All temporary and permanent employment reductions per establishment are summed up over the available quarters (or months). The data are categorized as to whether the establishments are stable or growing, contracting, or bankrupt; by Standard Industrial Classification (SIC) code; and by size as measured by average employment.

## Stable or Growing Establishments Versus Contracting or Bankrupt Establishments

The first sample consisted of 101,169 establishments with 20 quarters of continuous employment and also bankrupt establishments. This

**Figure 3.1    Employment Changes: Permanent Change from *A* to *B***

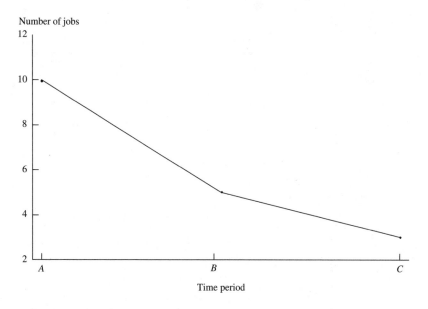

**Figure 3.2    Employment Changes: Permanent Change from *A* to *C***

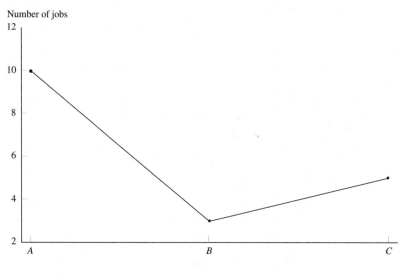

**Figure 3.3    Employment Changes: Temporary Change from *A* to *B***

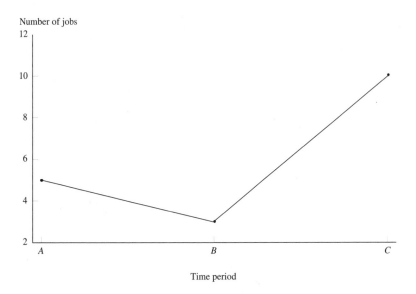

sample was used to categorize the establishments as (1) stable or grow-ing, (2) contracting, or (3) bankrupt. To determine whether establish-ments were stable or growing, or contracting, the log of quarterly employment (20 observations) was regressed on a time trend and four seasonal dummies (the constant was suppressed). If the coefficient on the time trend was negative with a $t$ statistic greater than one, the estab-lishment was categorized as having declining employment. If, on the other hand, the coefficient on the time trend was zero or positive with a $t$ statistic greater than or less than one, or negative with a $t$ statistic less than one, the establishment was categorized as having stable or grow-ing employment.

Reductions in employment were calculated using three consecutive quarters so that if employment declined between the first and second quarters in question, the third quarter was used to assess whether the reduction was permanent or temporary. The calculation continued for each successive quarter (i.e., second quarter vis-à-vis the third and fourth) and summed over 18 quarters. This three-quarter time period seems appropriate because UI benefits are available for only 26 weeks. If an employer seeks to recall a layoff, it is logical for this to occur prior to the exhaustion of benefits.

To ascertain the sensitivity of the analysis to the assumed time period, the calculation was repeated using five quarters. Employment in the first quarter was compared to that in the third. If employment declined in this period, then the fifth quarter was used to determine whether the decrease was permanent or temporary. Again, the employment reductions were summed over the 16 available quarters.

Confirming the work of Murphy and Topel (1987), tables 3.1 and 3.2 provide summaries showing that (1) more than half of employment reductions were permanent in the three categories of establishments using both the three-quarter and five-quarter time horizons, and (2) there is an increasing percentage of permanent employment reductions as the unemployment rate rises. The results for stable or growing establishments are somewhat sensitive to the choice of time horizon. There exists a 14 percentage point difference in the three-quarter and five-quarter results as compared to a mere 3 percentage point difference in the other two classifications. Regardless, the data reveal that permanent employment reductions are consistently more important than temporary reductions in all categories, particularly for contracting and bankrupt establishments, as expected.

**Table 3.1    Percentage of Permanent Employment Reductions by Type of Establishment (Texas, 1978-1982)**

| Time horizon | Establishments | | |
| --- | --- | --- | --- |
| | **Stable or growing** | **Contracting** | **Bankrupt** |
| | **Percent** | | |
| 3 quarters | 68 | 84 | 82 |
| 5 quarters | 54 | 81 | 79 |
| | **Number** | | |
| Establishments | 70,146 | 30,261 | 762 |

SOURCE: Data sample for 1978-1982 from Texas Employment Commission.
NOTE: The percentage of permanent employment reductions is calculated as the number of permanent employment reductions divided by total employment reductions times 100.

**Table 3.2  Permanent Employment Reductions and the Unemployment Rate (Texas, 1978-1989)**

|  | Year | | |
|---|---|---|---|
|  | **1979** | **1980** | **1981** |
|  | (%) | (%) | (%) |
| U.S. unemployment rate | 5.8 | 7.1 | 7.6 |
| Texas unemployment rate | 4.2 | 5.2 | 5.3 |
| Percentage of permanent employment reductions | 69.7 | 70.8 | 72.7 |

SOURCE: U.S. Department of Labor, Texas Employment Commission.
NOTE: The percentage of permanent employment reductions is calculated as the number of permanent employment reductions divided by total employment reductions times 100. Calculations are based on the data sample used in table 3.1.

## The Importance of Permanent Versus Temporary Reductions by SIC and Size of Firm

Do employment reductions differ by industry classification or by size of establishment? We analyzed the second set of data from the Texas Employment Commission records to answer these questions. Given the availability of monthly employment figures, six-month and nine-month time horizons were utilized.

Some records of individual establishments contained zero monthly employment numbers within periods of positive employment. It was not known whether the zero job figures were caused by establishment closings for those months or by nonreporting of employment to the Commission. To overcome this problem, the analysis was carried out using three separate methods:

1. The first method assumes that the zero employment numbers were caused by establishment closings.

2. If, in the period over which the employment reduction is assessed, the change in employment becomes positive again, method 2 ignores the zero employment figure, assuming it to have been due to the nonreporting of data. If employment does not recover in the

relevant time period, then a permanent decline in employment is assumed to have occurred, caused by the establishment closing.

3. Method 3 removes from the analysis those firms with spells of zero employment of duration shorter than the time period over which the employment reduction is assessed.

For both methods 2 and 3 assume that a brief zero employment spell is likely to reflect a reporting error, whereas a lengthy spell is most likely attributable to an actual establishment closing.

All three methods were analyzed using a six-month horizon. Method 2 was also analyzed using a nine-month horizon to discover the sensitivity of the results to the chosen assumptions.

Table 3.3 summarizes the results of the three methods by industry classification. Again, in all classifications, temporary employment reductions are far less important than those that are permanent.

The results of methods 1 and 2 are based on all 822,713 establishments, while those of method 3 represent 614,479 establishments (or 75 percent of the population). Not surprisingly for this time period, those classifications with typically stable employment—finance, real estate, and insurance, and general government—have the highest percentage of permanent employment reductions. Note that there is very little deviation in the results when establishments are analyzed in the aggregate. The importance of permanent declines ranges only from 62 to 64 percent. Within some classifications, however, there are substantial deviations in the results of the three methods. The largest occurs in the finance, real estate, and insurance category, where there is an 11 percentage point differential between the results of method 2 (6 months) and method 3.

Establishments with fewer than 100 employees account for approximately 98 percent of all establishments in the study population. Table 3.4 indicates that these establishments consistently show a lower percentage of permanent employment reductions than the other size groups. Given the overall percentage of permanent employment declines for all establishments in table 3.4 (approximately 62 percent), it is clear that the sheer number of smaller establishments conceals the high percentage of employment declines in larger establishments.

Table 3.3  Permanent Employment Reductions by Industry Classification (Texas, 1978–1989)

| Industry | Method 1 6 months (%) | Method 2 6 months (%) | Method 2 9 months (%) | Method 3 6 months (%) |
|---|---|---|---|---|
| Agriculture, forestry, and fishery | 70 | 75 | 66 | 72 |
| Mining, quarrying, and construction | 64 | 68 | 62 | 66 |
| Manufacturing | 56 | 66 | 57 | 66 |
| Transportation, utilities, and communications | 59 | 67 | 62 | 64 |
| Trade | 60 | 65 | 58 | 60 |
| Finance, real estate, and insurance | 70 | 79 | 75 | 68 |
| Services | 63 | 70 | 64 | 64 |
| General government | 71 | 79 | 73 | 79 |
| Bankruptcies | 60 | 67 | 60 | 64 |
| All establishments | 62 | 64 | 62 | 64 |

SOURCE: Based on UI-covered establishment data from 1978 to 1989 from the Texas Employment Commission.
NOTE: The percentage of permanent employment reductions is calculated as the number of permanent employment reductions divided by total employment reductions times 100.

Using method 2 (6 months), the larger establishments exhibit permanent employment reductions of 80 percent, while the smaller establishments exhibit only a 61 percent figure.

Table 3.4    Permanent Employment Reductions by Size of Establishment
(Texas, 1978–1989)

| Number of employees | Method 1 6 months (%) | Method 2 6 months (%) | Method 2 9 months (%) | Method 3 6 months (%) |
|---|---|---|---|---|
| Under 100 | 61 | 61 | 53 | 60 |
| 101–500 | 70 | 70 | 63 | 66 |
| 501–1,000 | 79 | 79 | 75 | 71 |
| 1,001–2,000 | 73 | 80 | 77 | 73 |
| 2,001–5,000 | 80 | 80 | 77 | 74 |
| Over 5,000 | 79 | 79 | 75 | 73 |

SOURCE: Based on UI-covered establishment data from 1978 to 1989 from the Texas Employment Commission.
NOTE: The percentage of permanent employment reductions is calculated as the number of permanent employment reductions divided by total employment reductions times 100.

Within size classifications, the largest deviation of 8 percent occurs in the smallest classification between methods 1 and 2 (9 months) and also between methods 2 (6 months) and 2 (9 months), and, in the 501-1,000 classification, between methods 1 and 3 and between methods 2 (6 months) and 3.[6]

## Concluding Remarks

The determination of the appropriate theoretical model of how the costs of unemployment benefits should be optimally allocated hinges on the relative importance of insured temporary and permanent layoffs. The measure of permanent employment reductions is only a proxy for insured permanent layoffs. However, the sheer magnitude of the results suggests that, even if insured permanent layoffs represent only half of the permanent employment reductions, they are substantial enough not to be overlooked.

# NOTES

1. In 1978, employment at firms in the sample was 2,602,410, as compared with total employment at all firms in Texas of 4,306,277 (see *Employment and Training Handbook* No. 394, p.476).

2. Note that Murphy and Topel (1987) use information on spells in progress. Thus, some layoffs that are counted as temporary could well be permanent, ex post.

3. As an example, suppose that there are 38 temporary layoffs, 52 permanent layoffs, and 10 quits. With quits included as a permanent decline, the percentage of permanent employment declines is 62 percent. If we exclude quits, the calculation is 58 percent (52/90).

4. This special relationship may not be permanently broken when the worker is unable to find work elsewhere (i.e. during a major downturn). UI allows for an additional 13 weeks of extended benefits.

5. Note that we are only calculating employment declines, rather than increases in employment.

6. One might conjecture that the lower percentage of permanent employment reductions for the smallest establishment size classification could stem from the growth of small establishments. Hence, age may be important. The data did not afford the opportunity to classify establishments by age.

# 4
# Funding Reemployment Costs
# When Job Losses are Permanent

Most of the previous theoretical writing on experience rating in unemployment insurance (UI) has been concerned with temporary layoffs and unemployment. The literature seems to provide no detailed theoretical analyses of the role of experience rating in UI when layoffs are permanent.[1] Permanent layoffs necessitate the transfer of workers from a contracting to another expanding sector (or into nonparticipation) and such moves involve costs such as those caused by retraining and geographic relocation. Presumably, UI is designed to cover some or all of these costs. The question arises as to who should be responsible for payment of these costs, or, alternatively, how should the system be experience rated?

In this chapter, we attempt to answer these questions by analyzing how the costs of permanent employment reductions ought to be allocated in order to achieve a specified socially optimal objective. An intuitive explanation of the economic model used in the analysis is presented in the body of the chapter. Alternatively, readers who prefer a presentation that also includes a more technical exposition are referred to the chapter appendix (which covers the material in the next three sections) and then to the concluding section of this chapter.

The general structure of the analysis is described in the remainder of this section. In the following section, the socially optimal rate of permanent layoffs is derived. The third section provides the analysis of permanent layoffs in the framework of market economies using four different methods of paying for the costs, i.e., via displaced workers, employers in the contracting sector, employers in the expanding sector, and the government. The consequences of the four assumptions are then determined. In the fourth section, the theoretical framework is made more realistic by introducing an explicit "waiting," "queuing," or "training" period through which laid-off workers must pass before they can relocate to another job. This period lengthens as total layoffs increase. Our findings are summarized in the final section.

In order to focus on the essential issue, the basic structure of the analysis is quite simple. There are only two sectors (or industries): one produces output X, and the other produces output Y. Labor is the only factor of production, and the *total* labor supply in the economy is fixed, although labor can move between the two sectors. In much of the analysis, there is no explicit unemployment, so that the sum of employment in both sectors equals total employment.

Initially, this economy is in equilibrium, in the sense that a unit of labor generates the same marginal utility (that is, the same additional value or well-being) for the representative consumer in either industry X or industry Y. Suppose, however, that this initial equilibrium is disturbed by a change in tastes towards good Y, which raises its marginal utility. As a result, consumers want more of good Y and less of good X.

To satisfy this new preference, a shift of workers from the production of good X to the production of good Y is required. However, moving these workers is not costless. If it were, the flow of workers to the Y sector would take place instantaneously. The costs of adjustment are associated with such factors as unemployment compensation, searching for a new job, retraining, and geographic relocation, and are incurred by the former employer, the employee, the government, or the new employer. Unemployment compensation constitutes a substantial proportion of these costs. The faster the flow of labor from sector X to sector Y, the higher are both the total and marginal costs of the employment adjustment. This basic model of an economy sets the stage for the analysis that follows.

## The Socially Optimal Rate of Permanent Layoffs

We now assume that there is a benevolent dictator who seeks to maximize the representative consumer's utility but recognizes that there are adjustment costs. The dictator is responsible for moving labor from sector X to sector Y at a socially optimal rate. That is, the benevolent dictator wishes to maximize the utility derived from the consumption of X and Y, adjusted for the costs of transferring labor from sector X to sector Y. Since the adjustment takes time, it is the present value of present and future net utilities, not the instantaneous level of net utility, that should be maximized.

The economy is in equilibrium initially, but, with the change in tastes, a marginal unit of labor now generates more utility in sector $Y$ than in sector $X$. In the presence of adjustment costs, how fast should the benevolent dictator shift labor from sector $X$ to sector $Y$?

The marginal cost of shifting an extra unit of labor from sector $X$ to sector $Y$ is equal to the marginal adjustment cost. The marginal benefit of moving this unit of labor is the excess of the extra utility gained from its employment in industry $Y$ over the utility lost in industry $X$. As more of good $Y$ is produced, its marginal utility declines, and as less of good $X$ is produced, its marginal utility rises. In other words, the consumer places less value on the consumption of additional units of a particular good. Thus, the marginal benefit of increasing employment in sector $Y$ declines as more and more labor is moved from sector $X$ to sector $Y$.

Since labor is moved gradually, this net benefit accrues not only in one period but over all periods until the new equilibrium is reached. The future benefits must be discounted at the social rate of discount and then summed over all periods. For the dictator's actions to be socially optimal, the present value of the net marginal benefits of moving one unit of labor must be equal to the marginal adjustment costs.

The optimal rate of adjustment of employment in sectors $X$ and $Y$ is rapid at first but then slows down until the new long-run equilibrium is reached. This is so because initially, as labor is shifted from industry $X$ to industry $Y$, the net benefit derived from transferring labor is high, and thus the flow of labor is high. As the marginal benefit of the labor transfer declines, the flow of labor also declines.

## Adjustment Paths in Market Economies

Let us now postulate the existence of output, labor, and capital markets and examine how adjustment to the new long-run equilibrium would take place. Four versions of the competitive model are analyzed. They differ in the assumptions about which agents are responsible for the payment of the adjustment costs. In case A, the workers who move from industry $X$ to industry $Y$ have to pay for these costs. In case B, the employers in the contracting industry $X$ bear the payment responsibility. In case C, the employers in the expanding sector $Y$ are required to pay for the costs of moving labor. Finally, in case D, a third party, such as the government, pays the adjustment costs but does not actually control the movement of labor from industry $X$ to industry $Y$.

### Case A: Displaced Workers Pay the Adjustment Costs

In a perfectly competitive market, employees are paid the value of their marginal product; that is, the wage is equal to the price of the product times the marginal product of the last worker hired. For example, if good $Y$ sells for $5 and the last worker hired produces three units of $Y$ in an hour, the wage in industry $Y$ is equal to $15 an hour. Of course, the marginal product of all previous workers hired is higher than that of the last worker because of diminishing marginal productivity of labor.

Since labor is assumed to be homogeneous, long-run equilibrium requires that the wage in the $X$ industry be equal to the wage in the $Y$ industry. In other words, there is no incentive for workers to move from one sector to the other.

As before, the economy's initial equilibrium is disturbed by a shift in tastes, which raises the marginal utility of good $Y$. In competitive markets, the price of good $X$ and the wage in industry $X$ fall in relation to those in industry $Y$, so that now wages in industry $Y$ are higher. With no adjustment costs, labor would move immediately from sector $X$ to sector $Y$, which would reestablish the equality of the two wage rates. With adjustment costs, however, workers in industry $X$ face two options. They may stay in that sector and receive a relatively low income stream. Alternatively, these workers may move to industry $Y$ and, for some time, receive a relatively high income stream.

Workers, however, cannot obtain the high income stream of industry $Y$ without paying the costs of moving. Let the price of moving be equal to the marginal adjustment cost. Thus, an individual worker will move when total earnings in industry $Y$ (properly discounted) exceed total earnings in industry $X$ by more than the cost of moving. The optimal rate of movement is obtained when the marginal worker is indifferent between staying in one sector and moving to the other. It can be shown that the conditions for the optimal transfer of labor from sector $X$ to sector $Y$ under a benevolent dictator and under the present competitive conditions, respectively, are equivalent. (See the chapter appendix for the formal proof.)

Having established that the flow of labor from sector $X$ to sector $Y$ is socially optimal, under the assumed circumstances, now consider what happens to the incomes of workers and employers. First, all initial employees in sector $X$ lose income in relation to the income earned by employees in sector $Y$. This loss is equal to the (properly discounted) difference between the wages in the two industries. Employees who remain in sector $X$ receive the lower wage, and employees who move to sector $Y$ receive the higher wage but must pay the adjustment cost. After proper discounting, the adjustment cost is just equal to the remaining difference between the wage in industry $Y$ and the wage in industry $X$ in the long run.

Second, what happens to nonlabor incomes in industry $X$? The representative firm's gross revenue per employee is equal to the price of good $X$ times the *average* product of labor (average output produced per worker). Since the firm's wage per employee is equal to the price of $X$ times the *marginal* product of labor, the firm's total nonlabor income (per employee) in any one year is equal to the price of good $X$ times the difference between the average product and marginal product of labor.

In accordance with the theory of the firm, let us assume that

1. the average product of labor is greater than or equal to the marginal product of labor,

2. both the average product of labor and the marginal product of labor are falling as employment in industry $X$ rises, and

3. the marginal product of labor falls faster than the average product of labor, resulting in an increase in the difference between the average product and marginal product as employment in sector $X$ rises.

Initially, the relative price of $X$ falls, and thus nonlabor income must fall. Afterwards, however, employment in sector $X$ falls, the price of $X$ rises, and the difference between the average and marginal product of labor falls, which means that nonlabor income may increase or decrease. The precise path of nonlabor income depends on the parameter values of the production and utility functions. However, it seems reasonable and realistic to assume that the net present value of the change in nonlabor income during the entire adjustment period is negative.

The third dimension is the income of workers in sector $Y$. Initially, employment in the industry rises, and so the marginal productivity of labor declines. This means that the real wage falls. It need not, however, fall in terms of the real purchasing power of *both* $X$ and $Y$. Employees initially in sector $Y$ enjoy a higher income during the adjustment period than do those in sector $X$.

Finally, consider the industry's nonlabor income, which is given by the difference between the average and marginal products of labor in sector $Y$ times employment in this sector. Initially, employment in the industry begins to rise, which, in turn, raises the difference between the average and marginal products of labor. Hence, nonlabor income must rise.

The discussion in this section thus far has been based on the assumption that wages in industry $X$ are flexible. Since wage and price stickiness seems to be quite common in many actual economies, we will address briefly what might happen when the wage in sector $X$ remains at its original level, while the value of the marginal product falls initially. Profit maximization by employers in industry $X$ would require the layoff of some employees, in order for the value of the marginal product to equal that initial sticky wage. This means that output of $X$ falls and that both the price of good $X$ and the marginal product of labor in this industry rise. In contrast to the previous adjustments, however, employment and output in sector $Y$ do not increase.

Unemployed workers in industry $X$ now evaluate two alternatives. First, they may search for a job in their industry and, if successful, displace another employee and earn the initial wage. Second, they may pay the adjustment costs, relocate to sector $Y$ and earn the wage there. If unemployed workers maximize their net expected incomes, they will be indifferent between remaining in sector $X$ and moving to sector $Y$ when the marginal adjustment costs equal the net present value of the difference between the wage in industry $Y$ minus the product of the wage in industry $X$ and the probability that the unemployed worker can find a job in industry $X$. This condition is not identical to that of the benevolent dictator. In particular, it has often been suggested that laid-off employees may be overly optimistic about finding a job in their own sector, especially when many layoffs are temporary. This would result in an overestimate of the probability of finding a job in industry X, which, in turn, would imply a suboptimal flow of labor to the other sector.

There is another reason why this flow of labor may be suboptimal in case A. It is very likely that unemployed workers face imperfect capital markets so that, for instance, they may not be able to borrow funds to finance the adjustment costs. In that situation, the movement of workers from sector X to sector Y would be lower than the socially optimal flow. (The appendix provides a more rigorous discussion of this point.)

### Case B: Employers in the Contracting Industry Bear the Adjustment Costs

We now turn to a different regime of paying for the adjustment costs. In particular, by law or by custom, the employers in the contracting sector X are fully responsible for this payment for all employees who separate from the sector.

An employer in this industry faces the situation in which, initially, the price of X falls, so that the value of the marginal product of labor also falls. If the wage does not decline by an equal amount, the employer lays off workers. However, the employer now has to pay the costs of moving labor to sector Y. Hence, the layoff decision is determined not only by the difference between the value of the marginal product and the wage, but also by the adjustment costs. Specifically, a profit-maximizing employer will lay off a marginal worker when the associated present and future labor cost savings exceed the marginal adjustment costs.

What is the level of the wage rate in industry X? Since firms in this sector are responsible for the adjustment costs of all workers who move (whether due to layoffs or to voluntary quits), the wage tends to equality with the wage paid in sector Y. To see why this is so, consider the circumstance in which initially the wage in industry X is less than the wage in industry Y. All employees in sector X then wish to be moved because they can earn a higher wage in the other industry and all costs of moving are paid by firms in sector X. This, however, would entail great total adjustment costs for employers in sector X, who are, therefore, induced to maintain their wages at the level of the $Y$ sector. In that case, employees in industry $X$ are indifferent between (1) staying, and (2) being laid off and moving to industry $Y$.

Firms in sector $X$ initiate layoffs and transfers of labor to sector $Y$. Thus, the system is in equilibrium when the rate of layoffs implies marginal adjustment costs equal to the present value of the difference between the value of the marginal product (wage) in sector $Y$ and the value of the marginal product of labor (which is less than the wage) in sector $X$. This is the same socially optimal rate of flow of labor from sector $X$ to sector $Y$ that occurred with the benevolent dictator.

The marginal product of labor in sector $Y$ determines *both* industries' wages. As labor flows from sector $X$ to sector $Y$, the marginal product of labor in sector $Y$ and wages in both sectors gradually fall until the new long-run level of wages is attained.

What are the implications of case B for the distribution of income? Since workers in both industries receive identical real wages, there is no change in the *relative* distribution of wage incomes. Compared with case A, however, workers in industry $X$ receive a higher real wage and workers in industry $Y$ receive the same real wage.

Firms in sector $X$ must now pay the adjustment costs. However, compared with case A, there are further costs. Nonlabor income in industry $X$ is reduced: first, employers must pay the adjustment costs, and, second, employers must continue to pay the relatively high wage of industry $Y$ despite the decline in the value of labor's marginal product in industry $X$. With employers in sector $X$ paying for the adjustment costs, nonlabor incomes in sector $Y$ tend to rise, as in case A.

### Case C: Employers in the Expanding Industry
### Bear the Adjustment Costs

In this situation, by custom or law, employers in the expanding sector $Y$ are obliged to bear the costs of transferring labor to their industry. As before, the marginal utility of $Y$ rises initially. Firms in the expanding sector hire workers in sector $X$ at the industry $Y$ wage, pay the moving costs, and then employ this labor. Employers will engage in this practice as long as the marginal adjustment cost is less than the present value of the difference between the value of the marginal product and the wage in industry $Y$.

What is the wage for workers who have moved from sector $X$ and are now working in sector $Y$? Competition among the employers in sector $Y$ ensures that wages are equal to the marginal productivity of labor in that industry, no matter where the workers originated or who paid the adjustment costs. It is only under imperfectly competitive conditions that the wage of the newly hired workers in industry $Y$ may fall short of marginal productivity. For instance, it may be possible that employers in sector $Y$ can contractually bind individuals from sector $X$ to work at a wage less than marginal productivity, in return for the employers' paying the moving costs. However, such indenture contracts are rarely enforceable in courts of law.

Since the wage in industry $Y$ for the newly hired workers is likely to exceed the value of the marginal product in industry $X$ and may well be equal to the value of the marginal product in industry $Y$, we conclude that the equilibrium condition is typically not the same as the socially optimal condition. Specifically, the adjustment rate is less than the socially optimal one. When employers in sector $Y$ behave competitively in the labor market, the profit-maximizing flow of labor from one sector to the other is zero. In other words, when employers in sector $Y$ must pay their transferred workers the full value of the marginal product in sector $Y$ in addition to the adjustment costs, they have no motive for hiring them and no labor will be transferred.

It may be worth noting that regulations requiring employers in the expanding sector to pay for the adjustment costs cannot be implemented easily. It is hard to identify employees who have moved from contracting sectors. Further, a tax or charge on new hires would have undesirable, negative incentive effects.

### Case D: Government Bears the Adjustment Costs

In the last three subsections, we have examined situations in which the adjustment costs are internalized to employers or employees who also control the rate of flow of labor. We now postulate crucially different circumstances, whereby the government, without direct control over the number of layoffs, pays the adjustment costs for any worker who has been laid off permanently in sector $X$. The adjustment costs are paid from general revenues, which, in turn, are financed by general taxes or by borrowing. None of these taxes, however, is linked directly to employers' or employees' layoff, hiring, or moving decisions.

As before, the marginal utility of good $Y$ rises, leading to a decline in the relative price of good $X$ and in the value of the marginal product of labor in $X$. The wage in sector $X$, however, remains equal to the wage in sector $Y$. Layoffs are costless to employers in sector $X$; thus, workers are laid off immediately, maintaining the equality of the value of the marginal products in both sectors. The government pays, more or less immediately, the adjustment costs for all layoffs and requires that workers relocate to the other sector. The new equilibrium is achieved virtually instantaneously. Given our basic assumption of rising marginal adjustment costs, this instantaneous adjustment would be nonoptimally fast and very costly. Alternatively, if the government somehow were to ration the payments of the adjustment costs, structural unemployment would likely result.

## From Theory to Practice

The theoretical framework of the previous sections is now modified in order to approximate current UI practices. In all states, qualified workers receive weekly unemployment benefits for the period of their joblessness (subject to a maximum duration of normally 26 weeks). In the preceding theoretical approach, by contrast, unemployment is ruled out, for the most part, because workers are transferred to sector $Y$ immediately upon layoff and/or payment of the marginal adjustment cost. In order to account for unemployment explicitly, we now postulate that the relocation process consists of a time of joblessness during which employees, who have left sector $X$, search for or wait for work in sector $Y$. The length of this unemployment period cannot be influenced by individual workers, but it lengthens with the *total* number of workers who leave the contracting sector.

Consider again case A, in which laid-off employees bear the costs of unemployment as well as any additional financial costs of moving from sector $X$ to sector $Y$. Further, wages in both industries are fully flexible and adjust to their respective marginal products at all times. Employees in sector $X$ have the choice of (1) remaining in the sector and receiving that wage, or (2) leaving the sector, waiting for a period of D, and then receiving the wage in sector $Y$ minus the cost of transferring between industries.

If, initially, the switch to sector $Y$ yields a higher net present value of future earnings minus the adjustment costs than staying in sector $X$, individual workers will move. As more and more do so, the unemployment duration and the additional adjustment costs rise. The earnings stream in sector $Y$ is postponed, and thus the net present value of these earnings falls. The costs of adjustment rise until the equilibrium rate of transfer is reached; this occurs when individual workers are indifferent between staying in or leaving sector $X$.

The marginal adjustment costs are now the sum of the net present value of the wages foregone in sector $Y$ because of the waiting period and any additional financial adjustment costs. In this case, the equilibrium rate of transfer of labor is identical to that of the socially optimal rate.

A UI system is now introduced in which unemployment benefits are paid to laid-off workers and are usually charged partially to the recipients' previous employers in sector $X$. In the theory of case B in the preceding section, the firms in the contracting sector are directly responsible for *both* the implementation and the costs of relocation. In practice, however, employers only make layoff decisions, and, with the present assumptions, laid-off employees relocate to a new job after a waiting or searching period and paying an additional financial adjustment cost. While on layoff, up to a maximum duration, workers receive weekly unemployment benefits. Does the current experience-rating system induce firms to lay off workers (permanently) at a rate equal to the socially optimal rate of transfer?

The firm's layoff decision can be presented formally as follows. Usually, firms are required to pay only some proportion of the UI benefits received by their laid-off workers. Thus, only a fraction of the present value of the benefits received by the laid-off worker represents the marginal tax costs of layoffs to the typical firm in the declining sector.

The marginal benefits from layoffs that accrue to the firm are the net present value of the difference between the wage and the value of the marginal product. The firm lays off workers as long as the marginal tax costs of layoffs are less than their marginal benefits. As the layoffs of the representative firm and thus total layoffs increase, there is an increase in unemployment duration and consequently in the present value of the UI benefits received by the laid-off workers. With a partially experience-rated tax rate, the firm's marginal tax costs of layoffs will, therefore, rise. The firm's optimal layoffs occur when these marginal tax costs are just equal to the marginal benefits of layoffs.

To understand whether the firm's optimal layoff is also the socially optimal one, the wage rate in sector $X$ needs to be ascertained. This determination is made in the framework of two alternative assumptions. First, it is assumed that markets are perfect, so that wages in sector $X$ are flexible. The second approach is to assume that wages in sector $X$ are inflexible and are equal to wages in sector $Y$.

When the wage rates in industry $X$ are flexible, their present value must be determined by the equality of the properly discounted income streams in sectors $X$ and $Y$. In particular, the present value of wages in industry $X$ must equal the present value of earnings in industry $Y$ (after the period of unemployment), plus the unemployment benefits, less the financial costs of transferring to industry $Y$.

What determines the layoff rate of the employer? In this case, the employer does not pay the full cost of the UI benefits, but only a fraction thereof, and the unemployment benefits are less than the wage in sector $Y$ (typically, benefits are 40 to 60 percent of wages). The resulting layoff rate will be higher than the socially optimal rate because the latter imposes the full adjustment cost on the employer. Thus, imperfect experience rating leads to higher-than-optimal layoffs by firms, resulting in higher-than-optimal levels of unemployment. Increases in the degree of experience rating would reduce the firm's layoff rate and bring it closer to the socially optimal one.

Under the second set of conditions, the relative wages in sector $X$ are inflexible and are equal to the wages in sector $Y$. With the current assumptions, the optimal transfer of labor from industry $X$ to industry $Y$ requires that the present value of the proportion of unemployment benefits paid by the employer be equal to the present value of the wage in sector $Y$ from the time of layoff to the time of hire in that sector plus any additional costs of transfer. The profit-maximizing layoff decision leads to layoffs and an unemployment duration that are in excess of what is socially optimal. Socially optimal layoffs and unemployment duration may be achieved by raising the proportion of benefits charged to the employer or by raising unemployment benefits. For that purpose, the increase in benefits need not actually be paid to the unemployed workers. Its function is to raise the marginal costs of layoffs, so that the rate of layoffs and therefore the duration and level of unemployment are reduced toward their social optima.

## Summary and Conclusions

In this chapter, the role of experience rating in UI has been reexamined in the context of permanent layoffs. Previous investigations have been largely confined to temporary layoffs. Our main findings are as follows:

1. Socially optimal rates of labor transfer from contracting to expanding sectors can be achieved by charging the costs of transfer either to the (permanently) laid-off workers or to the employers in the contracting sector. Charging laid-off workers, however, requires fully flexible wages and perfect capital markets. When wages are sticky, charging employers may still achieve an optimal outcome.

2. Whoever is responsible for paying the transfer costs will suffer a loss of income (at least, in the short run).

3. Charging the transfer costs to employers in the expanding sector(s) would be socially optimal only if extremely complicated rules could be enforced. Consequently, we rule out this alternative.

4. Financing the transfer costs partially or wholly by a general tax would lead to nonoptimally high transfers or to high structural unemployment.

5. When wages are inflexible, employers are charged and experience rated imperfectly and the unemployment benefits fall short of wages. Then permanent layoffs tend to be larger than optimal. To achieve the optimal outcome in these cases, employer charges should be increased, even though they may exceed benefits.

Our general conclusion is that "full" experience rating is a highly desirable UI property for permanent, as well as for temporary, layoffs. Indeed, in some circumstances, the system ought to be "more than fully" experience rated to achieve the socially optimal adjustment. In practice, however, the goal of socially optimal transfers will, as always, be balanced against considerations of equity, that is, can the declining sector afford a higher UI tax?

## NOTES

1.As mentioned previosly, temporary layoffs are here defined as employment separations that are reversed by recalls or new hires after a relatively short period of time. Temporary, unlike permanent, layoffs do not lead to long-run reductions in the employer's workforce. Typical examples of the literature on temporary layoffs are Feldstein (1976), Wolcowitz (1984), and Cook (1992).

# Appendix to Chapter 4
## The Formal Two-Sector Model

The following sections mirror those in the body of the chapter but offer a formal presentation of the theoretical framework.

In this model, we assume initially that there is no explicit unemployment so that

$$N = N_x + N_y$$

where $N$ is the total labor force and $N_x$ and $N_y$ stand for employment in sectors $X$ and $Y$. The production functions in the two sectors are given by

$$X = g(N_x) \text{ and}$$
$$Y = h(N_y) = h(N - N_x).$$

The marginal products of labor in the two sectors, $MP_x(= g')$ and $MP_y(= h')$, are positive and declining, that is,

$$g' > 0, g'' < 0, \text{ and}$$
$$h' > 0, h'' < 0.$$

There is a representative consumer with a utility function,

$$U(X, Y).$$

The marginal utilities of goods $X$ and $Y$, $MU_x(= U_x)$ and $MU_y(= U_y)$, are positive and declining, that is,

$$U_x > 0, U_{xx} < 0, \text{ and}$$
$$U_y > 0, U_{yy} < 0.$$

It is also convenient to assume that the marginal utility of $X$ rises with the consumption of $Y$ and vice versa, that is,

$$U_{xy} > 0.$$

When employed in sector $X$, a unit of labor generates a marginal utility of $MU_x MP_x$; when employed in sector $Y$, a unit of labor generates a marginal utility of $MU_y MP_y$. Thus, the equilibrium condition is $MU_x MP_x = MU_y MP_y$. This condition can be derived formally by maximizing the utility function subject to the stated constraints:

$$\text{Max } U(X, Y)$$

subject to

$$X = g(N_x), Y = h(N_y) \text{ and } N_x + N_y = N.$$

The initial equilibrium can be illustrated by means of a simple diagram. Figure 4.1 includes a production possibilities curve (*PPC*) and an indifference curve ($I_1$), which is derived from the utility function of the representative consumer. Maximum utility is achieved at the point of tangency ($E_1$) of the two curves. This point is defined by the equality of the slope of the indifference curve, namely $MU_x / MU_y$, and the slope of the production possibilities curve, $MP_x / MP_y$.

The initial equilibrium $(E_1)$ is disturbed by an exogenous change in tastes, for example, which raises the marginal utility of Y. As a result, the new indifference curve is $I_2$, and the new long-run equilibrium is $E_2$, with increased levels of Y and $N_y$ and reduced levels of X and $N_x$.

**Figure 4.1    Equilibrium in the Two-Sector Model**

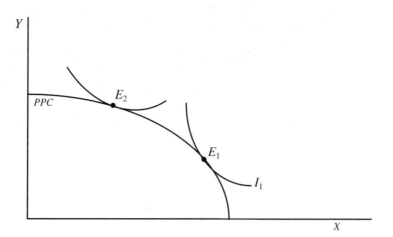

If the movement from $E_1$ to $E_2$ were costless, then the economy would shift to $E_2$ instantaneously. In the present model, however, there are adjustment costs that prevent an immediate adjustment. Unemployment compensation constitutes a substantial proportion of these adjustment costs in the case of permanent layoffs.

There is a flow of labor $(\dot{N})$ from sector X to sector Y. It is plausible that faster adjustment involves both higher total and higher marginal costs of adjustment. Consequently, we assume that the adjustment cost function is similar to that in figure 4.2. When adjustment is zero, both total and marginal adjustment costs are zero. As the rate of adjustment increases, both the height and the slope of the function rise. Formally, the properties of the adjustment cost function are stated as follows:

$f(\dot{N}) > 0$ for all $\dot{N} > 0$

when $f'(\dot{N}) > 0$, $f''(\dot{N}) > 0$ and

when $f(0) = 0$, $f'(0) = 0$.

**Figure 4.2    The Adjustment Cost Function**

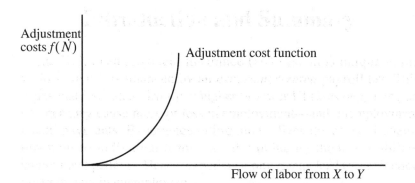

This type of adjustment cost is likely to cause a gradual adjustment from $E_1$ to $E_2$, because instantaneous adjustment would be prohibitively expensive.

**The Socially Optimal Rate of Permanent Layoffs**

We now assume that there is a benevolent dictator who wishes to maximize the utility of a representative consumer while recognizing the existence of adjustment costs.  The appropriate maximization problem can be stated formally as the exponential function:

$$(4.1) \quad \text{Max } V_t = \int_t^\infty [\, U\,(X_\tau, Y_\tau) - f\,(\dot{N}_\tau)\,]\, e^{-\rho\,(\tau - t)}\, d\tau$$

subject to: $X = g(N_x)$
$\qquad\qquad Y = h(N_y)$
$\qquad\qquad N = N_x + N_y.$

The letter $\rho$ stands for the social rate of discount, the adjustment costs $f(\dot{N})$ are measured in the same units as utility, and $e\ (= 2.71828)$ represents the discount function. Throughout this appendix, the following notation with respect to time indexes is maintained. A change in tastes (or technology) occurs at time $t_0$. The subscript $t$ refers to any period including and subsequent to $t_0$ and the subscript $\tau$ refers to any period including and subsequent to $t$. In symbols, $t_0 < t < \tau < \infty.$[1] The preceding objective function states that the benevolent dictator wishes to maximize the utility derived from the consumption of $X$ and $Y$, adjusted for the costs of transferring labor from sector $X$ to sector $Y$. Since the adjustment takes time, it is the present value of present and future net utilities that should be maximized, not the instantaneous level of net utility. This present value is represented by $V_t$ in equation (4.1).

Initially, the economy is in equilibrium at point $E_1$ in figure 4.1. As mentioned, in this initial equilibrium $MU_x MP_x = MU_y MP_y$ (or $U_x g' = U_y h'$) and $f'(\dot{N}) = 0$ because $\dot{N} = 0$. At time $t_0$, there is a shift in tastes (or production technology) so that now $MU_y MP_y > MU_x MP_x$. In other words, a marginal unit of labor now generates more utility in sector $Y$ than in sector $X$. In the presence of adjustment costs, how fast should the benevolent dictator shift labor from sector $X$ to sector $Y$?

This maximization problem can be solved mathematically by standard techniques of optimal control theory. We favor the following slightly less formal and more heuristic solution. The marginal cost of shifting an extra unit of labor from sector $X$ to sector $Y$ is equal to the marginal adjustment cost, namely $f'(\dot{N})$. The marginal benefit of moving this unit of labor is the extra utility gained from its employment in industry $Y$ minus the utility lost in industry $X$. In any one period, this excess is measured by $(MU_y MP_y - MU_x MP_x)$ or, equivalently by $(U_y h' - U_x g')$. Since labor is moved gradually, this net benefit accrues not only in one period but over all periods until the new equilibrium ($E_2$ in figure 4.1) is reached. The future benefits must be discounted at the social rate of discount $\rho$ and then summed. For the dictator's actions to be socially optimal, the present value of the net marginal benefits of moving one unit of labor must be equal to the marginal adjustment costs. Formally, this condition can be stated as

$$(4.2) \quad f'(\dot{N}_t) = \int_t^{\infty} (MU_{y\tau} MP_{y\tau} - MU_{x\tau} MP_{x\tau}) e^{-\rho(\tau - t)} \, d\tau \,,$$

which must hold for all time periods after and including $t_0$, that is, for $t \geq t_0$. When this condition is differentiated with respect to time, the so-called Euler equation of the calculus of variations is obtained.

The optimal rate of adjustment of employment in sectors $X$ and $Y$ to the new equilibrium is illustrated in figure 4.3. Initially, $N_x$ is relatively high, and $N_y$ is relatively low. At $t_0$, the change in tastes occurs, and the benevolent dictator allocates labor according to equation (4.2). As illustrated in figure 4.3, the adjustment is rapid at first but then slows down until the new steady state is reached at $t^*$. As labor is shifted from sector $X$ to sector $Y$, the marginal product of labor rises in sector $X$ and falls in sector $Y$. Similarly, the marginal utility of $X$ rises and that of $Y$ falls. In other words, as labor is moved from $X$ to $Y$, $MU_x MP_x$ rises and $MU_y MP_y$ falls until, in the new steady state, they are again equal. Initially, the net benefit derived from transferring labor is high, and hence $\dot{N}$ is high. As $(MU_y MP_y - MU_x MP_x)$ declines, the flow of labor also declines.

**Figure 4.3    Optimal Employment Adjustment**

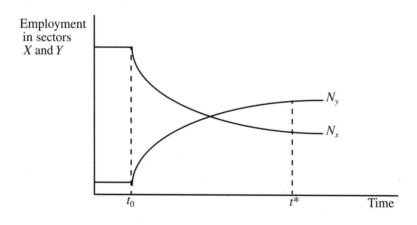

## Adjustment Paths in Market Economies

Here we include output, labor, and capital markets to examine how adjustment to the new steady state would take place. Four versions of the competitive model are studied; these are based on different assumptions about which agents are responsible for the payment of the adjustment costs.

In market models, prices ($P_x$ and $P_y$) and wages ($w_x$ and $w_y$) play an important role. For convenience, let $P_y$ be the numeraire, so that $P_y = 1$. Hence, factors such as wages, incomes, and adjustment costs are all measured in units of $Y$. The representative consumer maximizes his/her utility subject to a budget constraint. This implies the equality of the marginal rate of substitution with the price ratio, or

$$(4.3) \quad MU_x / MU_y = P_x.$$

Equation (4.3) is assumed to hold in all four versions of the market model, both during the adjustment periods and in the steady states.

### Case A: Displaced Workers Pay the Adjustment Costs

To begin, we postulate a perfectly competitive version of the model, such that employees are paid the values of their marginal products:

$$w_x = P_x MP_x \text{ and } w_y = MP_y.$$

These two conditions are satisfied both during the adjustment period and in steady states.

Since labor is assumed to be homogeneous, steady state equilibrium requires that $w_x = w_y$ or $P_x MP_x = MP_y$. After substituting for $P_x$ from equation (4.3), we obtain

$$MU_y/MU_x = MP_x/MP_y,$$

which is the tangency condition illustrated in figure 4.1.

As before, the economy's initial equilibrium is disturbed at time $t_0$ by a shift in tastes, which raises $MU_y$. In competitive markets, $P_x$ and $w_x$ fall relative to $P_y$ and $w_y$, so that now, $w_y > w_x$. With no adjustment costs, labor would move immediately from sector $X$ to sector $Y$ which would reestablish the equality of the two wage rates. Wage maximizing behavior by employees would establish the new equilibrium instantaneously at $E_2$ in figure 4.1. With adjustment costs, however, workers in industry $X$ face two options. They may stay in their industry and receive a relatively low income stream, which has a present value of

$$(4.4) \qquad NPV_{xt} = \int_t^\infty w_{x\tau} e^{-r(\tau - t)} d\tau,$$

where $r$ stands for a representative rate of interest at which future earnings are discounted. Alternatively, the workers in industry $X$ may move to industry $Y$ and receive a relatively high income stream, which has a present value of

$$(4.5) \qquad NPV_{yt} = \int_t^\infty w_{y\tau} e^{-r(\tau - t)} d\tau.$$

The workers cannot, however, obtain $NPV_{yt}$ without paying the costs of moving to industry $Y$. Let the price of moving be equal to the marginal adjustment cost. The individual worker will move if

$$(4.6) \qquad [NPV_{yt} - \phi'(\dot{N})] \geq NPV_{xt}$$

where $\phi'(\dot{N})$ stands for the marginal adjustment cost, measured in units of $Y$. Thus, an individual worker will move to industry $Y$ when total earnings in that sector (properly discounted) exceed total earnings in industry $X$ by more than the cost of moving. The optimal rate of movement is obtained when the marginal worker is indifferent between staying in industry $X$ and moving to industry $Y$, that is, when

$$(4.7) \qquad \phi'(\dot{N}_t) = \int_t^\infty (w_{y\tau} - w_{x\tau}) e^{-r(\tau - t)}$$

or, since wages are equal to the values of their marginal products:

$$(4.7') \quad \phi'(\dot{N}_t) = \int_t^\infty (MP_{y\tau} - P_{x\tau} MP_{x\tau}) e^{-r(\tau - t)} d\tau.$$

Equations (4.2) and (4.7'), which present the conditions for the optimal transfer of labor from sector $X$ to sector $Y$ under a benevolent dictator and under competitive conditions can be shown to be equivalent. First, substitute $MU_x / MU_y$ for $P_x$ in equation (4.7') and second, multiply the entire equation by $MU_y$. Then the left-hand side of the resulting equation is $MU_y \phi'(\dot{N}_t)$. Since $\phi'(\dot{N}_t)$ is the marginal adjustment cost measured in units of $Y$, while $f'(\dot{N}_t)$ is the same cost measured in utility units, it follows that

$$f'(\dot{N}_t) = MU_y \phi'(\dot{N}).$$

The only remaining difference between equations (4.2) and (4.7') is the rate of discount. In equation (4.2), it is $\rho$, the social rate of discount, while in equation (4.7'), it is $r$, the representative market rate of interest. If all markets, and in particular the capital market, are perfectly competitive, then the representative market rate of interest equals the social rate of discount. Thus, equations (4.2) and (4.7') are indeed equivalent and yield the same optimal rate of transfer of labor from sector $X$ to sector $Y$.

The optimal paths of labor in industry $X$ and industry $Y$ under competitive conditions are the same as those under the benevolent dictator and have already been illustrated in figure 4.3. Figure 4.4 illustrates the corresponding movement of wages in the two industries. The change in tastes at time $t_0$ reduces $P_x$ relative to $P_y$ and, hence, $w_x$ falls relative to $w_y$. Thereafter, as labor flows from sector $X$ to sector $Y$, output of $X$ falls and output of $Y$ rises, $MP_x$ rises and $MP_y$ falls, $MU_x$ rises and $MU_y$ falls, and $P_x$ rises relative to $P_y(= 1)$. This means that $w_x$ rises and $w_y$ falls until the new long-run equilibrium is established at time $t^*$ at which $w_x = w_y$.

Having determined that the flow of labor from sector $X$ to sector $Y$ (that is, $\dot{N}$) is socially optimal under the assumed circumstances, we now consider what happens to the incomes of workers and employers. First, all initial employees in sector $X$ lose income in relation to that earned by employees in sector $Y$. This loss is equal to the (properly discounted) area between the upper $w_y$ line and the lower $w_x$ line in figure 4.4. Employees who remain in industry $X$ receive the lower wage $w_x$, and employees who move to industry $Y$ receive the higher wage $w_y$ but must pay the adjustment cost, which, after proper discounting, is just equal to the remaining difference between $w_y$ and $w_x$. Thus, compared to workers in sector $Y$, each employee who is in sector $X$ at $t_0$ suffers an income loss between $t_0$ and $t^*$, which, in net present value terms, is equal to

$$(4.8) \quad \text{Workers' loss}_x = \int_{t_0}^{t^*} (w_{y\tau} - w_{x\tau}) \, e^{-r(\tau - t_0)} \, d\tau .$$

Second, what happens to nonlabor incomes in sector $X$? The representative firm's gross revenue per employee is $P_x AP_x$, where $AP_x$ stands for the *average product of labor*. Since the wage per employee is $P_x MP_x$, the firm's total nonlabor income in any one year is $P_x (AP_x - MP_x) N_x$.[2] In accordance with the standard theory of the firm, we assume that, over the relevant range of $N_x$

1. $AP_x \geq MP_x$

2. both $AP_x$ and $MP_x$ are falling with $N_x$

3. $MP_x$ falls faster than $AP_x$
   so that $(AP_x - MP_x)$ rises with $N_x$.

At time $t_0$, the relative price of $X$ (that is, $P_x$) falls, and, so nonlabor income must fall. After $t_0$, however, $N_x$ falls (see figure 4.3); hence $P_x$ rises, and $(AP_x - MP_x)$ falls, which means that nonlabor income may rise or fall. As discussed in chapter 4, we find it reasonable to assume that the net present value of the change in nonlabor income during the entire adjustment period is negative, although the parameter values of the production and utility functions determine the exact path of nonlabor income.

**Figure 4.4　Movement of Wages: Case A**

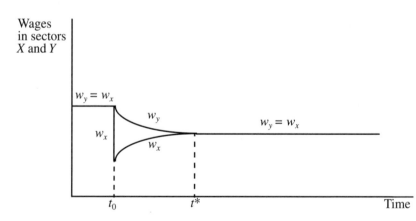

The third dimension is the income of workers in sector $Y$. Here the wage is $P_y MP_y$ per employee per period, where, as before, $P_y = 1$ (the numeraire).

Starting at $t_0$, $N_y$ rises and thus $MP_y$ declines. This means that the real wage, measured in terms of good $Y$, falls. However, it need not fall in terms of the real purchasing power over goods from *both* sector $X$ and sector $Y$. The path of $w_y$ in figure 4.4 shows that those employees who are in sector $Y$ at time $t_0$ enjoy a higher income during the adjustment period than do those in sector $X$.

Finally, consider nonlabor income in sector $Y$, which is given by $(AP_y - MP_y)N_y$. Let us assume, as before, that $AP_y \geq MP_y$ and that $(AP_y - MP_y)$ rises with increases in $N_y$. At time $t_0$, $N_y$ begins to rise, which, in turn, raises $(AP_y - MP_y)$. Hence, nonlabor income (measured in terms of $Y$) must rise.

The discussion in this section has so far been based on the assumption that wages in industry $X$ are flexible, in the sense that they are always equal to $P_x MP_x$. Since wage and price stickiness seems to be quite common in many actual economies, we will address briefly what might happen when the wage in sector $X$ remains at its initial level ($w_x^*$) while the value of the marginal product falls at $t_0$. Profit maximization by employers in industry $X$ would require that $\Delta N_x$ employees be laid off, so that the equality of $w_x^*$ and $P_x MP_x$ can be maintained. This means that output of industry $X$ falls and that both $P_x$ and $MP_x$ rise. In contrast to the previous adjustments, however, employment and output in industry $Y$ do not increase.

Unemployed workers in industry $X$ now consider two alternatives. First, they may search for a job in that sector, and, if successful, displace another employee and earn $w_x$. Second, they may pay the adjustment costs, relocate to industry $Y$, and earn $w_y$ ($= MP_y$). Let $Pr$ be the probability that an unemployed worker can find a job in sector $X$. If unemployed workers maximize their net expected incomes, they will be indifferent between remaining in sector $X$ and moving to sector $Y$ when

$$(4.9) \quad \phi'(\dot{N}) = \int_t^\infty MP_{y\tau} e^{-r(\tau - t)} d\tau - Pr\left[ \int_t^\infty w_x^* e^{-r(\tau - t)} d\tau \right].$$

This condition is not identical to those in equations (4.2) and (4.7'). In particular, it has often been suggested that laid-off employees in industry $X$ may be overly optimistic about finding a job in the sector, especially when many layoffs are temporary. This would result in an overestimate of $Pr$, which, in turn, would imply a suboptimal flow of labor from industry $X$ to industry $Y$.

There is another reason why the flow of labor may be suboptimal in case A. As has been pointed out in the discussion of equation (4.7'), for the latter to be an optimal decision rule, the market discount rate $r$ must equal the social rate of discount $\rho$; this equality would be ensured in perfect capital markets. However, it is very likely that unemployed workers face imperfect capital markets and that their discount rates exceed the social rate of discount. In that instance, the flow of labor from sector $X$ to sector $Y$ would be lower than the socially optimal flow.

### Case B: Employers in the Contracting Industry Bear the Adjustment Costs

We now assume that by law or by custom, employers in the contracting sector $X$ are fully responsible for the payment of the adjustment costs of all employees who separate from the sector. An employer in this industry faces the situation in which, at time $t_0$, the price of sector $X$ falls, so that the value of the marginal product of labor ($P_x MP_x$) also falls. If the wage $w_x$ does not decrease by an equal amount, the employer lays off workers. However, as stipulated, the employer now has to pay the costs of moving workers to industry $Y$. Thus, the layoff decision is determined not only by the difference between the value of the marginal product and the wage, but also by the adjustment costs. Specifically, a profit-maximizing employer will lay off a worker when the resulting present and future labor cost savings exceed the marginal adjustment costs. Formally, this condition can be written as

$$(4.10) \quad \phi'(\dot{N}_t) < \int_t^\infty (w_{x\tau} - P_{x\tau} MP_{x\tau}) e^{-r(\tau - t)} d\tau,$$

where, as in case A, all variables are measured in units of $Y$. The equilibrium rate of layoffs is obtained when the "<" is replaced by an "=" in equation (4.10).

What is the wage level in sector $X$, namely, $w_x$? Since firms in the industry are responsible for the adjustment costs of all workers who move (whether because of layoffs or voluntary quits), $w_x$ tends to equality with the wage paid in sector $Y$. To see why this is so, consider that initially $w_x < w_y$. All employees in industry $X$ then wish to be moved because they can earn a higher wage in industry $Y$ and all costs of moving are paid by firms in industry $X$. This, however, would entail great total adjustment costs for employers in sector $X$, who are, therefore, induced to maintain their wages at the level of $w_y$. In that situation, employees in sector $X$ are indifferent between (1) staying, and (2) being laid off and moving to sector $Y$. Firms in industry $X$ initiate layoffs and transfers of labor to industry $Y$. They do so at the rate $\dot{N}$, which is implied by

$$(4.11) \quad \phi'(\dot{N}_t) = \int_t^\infty (MP_y - P_{x\tau} MP_{x\tau}) e^{-r(\tau - t)} d\tau.$$

Thus, the system is in equilibrium when the rate of layoffs implies marginal adjustment costs equal to the present value of the difference between the value of the marginal product (= wage) in sector $Y$ and the value of the marginal product of labor in sector $X$.

Comparison of equations (4.2), (4.7'), and (4.11) shows that, after appropriate substitutions, they are all equivalent. All three imply the same socially optimal rate of flow of labor from sector $X$ to sector $Y$.

When equation (4.11) holds, then $P_x MP_x \leq w_x = w_y = MP_y$ throughout the adjustment period. The marginal product of labor in sector $Y$ determines *both* industries' wages. As labor flows from sector $X$ to sector $Y$, the marginal product of labor in sector $Y$ and wages in both sectors gradually fall until the new level of wages is attained at $t^*$. Figure 4.5 illustrates the movement of the wag-

**Figure 4.5    Movement of Wages: Case B**

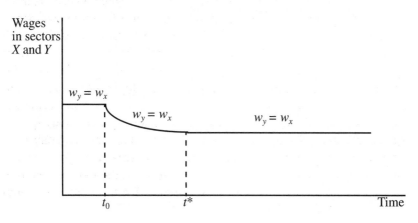

es.

What are the implications of case B for the distribution of income? Since workers in both sectors $X$ and $Y$ receive identical real wages, there is no change in the *relative* distribution of wage incomes. Compared with case A, however, workers in industry $X$ receive a higher real wage and workers in industry $Y$ receive the same real wage.

Firms in industry $X$ must now pay the total adjustment costs (TAC). In terms of net present value, these costs amount to

$$(4.12) \quad TAC = \int_{t_0}^{t^*} \phi'(\dot{N}_\tau) \, \dot{N}_\tau e^{-r(\tau - t_0)} \, d\tau,$$

where, as before, $\phi'(\dot{N})$ is the price per transfer and $\dot{N}$ is the number of transferred employees. However, as compared with case A, there are other costs. Prior to $t_0$, $P_x MP_x = MP_y$, so that nonlabor income is equal to $P_x(AP_x - MP_x)N_x = (P_x AP_x - MP_y)N_x$. At $t_0$, $P_x$ and, consequently, the value of the marginal product in industry $X$ fall. Firms in sector $X$, however, must continue to pay the wage in sector $Y$, namely, $w_y = MP_y \geq P_x MP_x$. Hence, after $t_0$, $(P_x AP_x - MP_y) \leq (P_x AP_x - P_x MP_x)$ and this inequality is maintained until the new equilibrium is established at $t^*$. Thus, compared with case A, nonlabor income in sector $X$ is reduced: first, employers must pay adjustment costs $TAC$ as defined by equation (4.12), and, second, employers must continue to pay the relatively high $Y$ industry wage ($w_y$) despite the decline in the value of labor's marginal product in $X$ (that is, $P_x MP_x$). As in case A, nonlabor incomes in sector $Y$ tend to increase when employers in sector $X$ pay for the adjustment costs.

### Case C: Employers in the Expanding Industry Bear the Adjustment Costs

In this situation, employers in the expanding sector $Y$ bear the costs of transferring labor from sector $X$. As before, the marginal utility of $Y$ rises in period $t_0$. Since by assumption, $P_y = 1$, this means that $P_x MP_x$ must be lower relative to $P_y MP_y$ and consequently $w_x$ must fall. Firms in the expanding sector $Y$ hire workers in sector $X$ at a wage of $\hat{w}_y$, pay the moving costs of $\phi'(\dot{N})$ per worker, and then employ these individuals in sector $Y$, where their contribution to production is $P_y MP_y$. Employers will engage in this practice as long as the marginal adjustment cost is less than the present value of the difference between the value of the marginal product in sector $Y$ and the wage $\hat{w}_y$. Thus, firms in industry $Y$ transfer the profit-maximizing number of workers from industry $X$ when the following condition is satisfied at any time after $t_0$:

$$(4.13) \qquad \phi'(\dot{N}_t) = \int_t^\infty (MP_{y\tau} - \hat{w}_{y\tau}) e^{-r(\tau - t)} d\tau .$$

What is the wage $\hat{w}_y$ for workers who have moved from sector $X$ and are now working in sector $Y$? Since the marginal product of old and newly arrived workers in sector $Y$ is equal to $MP_y$, competition among the employers in sector $Y$ ensures that wages must be such that $w_y = \hat{w}_y = MP_y$, no matter where the workers originated or who paid the adjustment costs. It is only under imperfectly competitive conditions that $\hat{w}_y$ may fall short of $MP_y$. For instance, it may be possible that employers in industry $Y$ can contractually bind workers from industry $X$ to work at a wage less than $MP_y$, in return for the payment of the moving costs by employers. Such indenture contracts are rarely enforceable in courts of law, however.

Since $\hat{w}_y$ is highly likely to exceed $P_x MP_x$ and may well be equal to $MP_y$, we conclude that equation (4.13) is typically not the same as equations (4.2), (4.7') or (4.11). Specifically, equation (4.13) tends to lead to an adjustment rate less than the socially optimal one. When employers in sector $Y$ behave competitively in the labor market, so that $\hat{w}_y = MP_y$, the profit-maximizing flow of labor from industry $X$ to industry $Y$ is zero.

### Case D: Government Bears the Adjustment Costs

In this situation, the government pays the adjustment costs for any worker laid off permanently in sector $X$, but it has no direct control over the number of layoffs. The adjustment costs are covered by general revenues that are financed by general taxes or by borrowing.

As before, at time $t_0$, $MU_y$ rises and thus $P_x$ and $P_x MP_x$ fall. The wage in sector $X$, however, remains at $w_y$. Layoffs are costless to sector $X$ employers, and $\Delta N$ workers are laid off immediately; $\Delta N$ must be such as to maintain the equality $w_y = P_x MP_x$. The government pays, more or less immediately, the adjustment costs for all layoffs and requires that workers relocate to sector $Y$. The new equilibrium (that is, point $E_2$ in figure 4.1) is achieved virtually instantaneously. Given our basic assumption of rising marginal adjustment costs, this instantaneous adjustment would be nonoptimally fast and very costly. In other words, equation (4.2) would not be satisfied.

### From Theory to Practice

We now assume that the relocation process consists of a period of unemployment during which employees, who have left sector $X$, search for or wait for their new jobs in sector $Y$. Further, the duration ($D$) of this period of unemployment lengthens with the *total* number of workers who leave the contracting sector.[3]

Consider again case A, in which laid-off employees bear the costs of unemployment as well as any additional financial costs of moving from sector $X$ to sector $Y$. Further, wages in both sectors are fully flexible and adjust to their respective marginal products, that is, $w_y = MP_y$ and $w_x = P_x MP_x$ at all times. Employees in sector $X$ have the choice of remaining in that industry and receiving the wage, as in equation (4.4), of $w_{xt} = P_{xt} MP_{xt}$, or of leaving sector $X$, waiting for a period $D$ (measured in years), and then receiving

$$(4.14) \quad NPV_{y(t+D)} - g'(\dot{N}) = \int_{t+D}^{\infty} w_{y\tau} e^{-r(\tau-t)} d\tau - g'(\dot{N}),$$

where $g'(\dot{N})$ represents any costs of moving to sector $Y$ additional to the cost of waiting, and $NPV_{y(t+D)}$ is the net present value at time $t$ of the wages earned in sector $Y$ from period $(t + D)$ onward.

If initially $[NPV_{y(t+D)} - g'(\dot{N})] > NPV_{xt}$, individual workers move from sector $X$ to sector $Y$. However, as more and more do so, the unemployment duration $D$ and the additional adjustment cost $g'(\dot{N})$ rise, and the earnings stream in sector $Y$ is postponed. Hence, $NPV_{y(t+D)}$ falls and $g'(\dot{N})$ rises until the equilibrium rate of transfer is reached when $[NPV_{y(t+D)} - g'(\dot{N})] = NPV_{xt}$, that is, when individual workers are indifferent between (1) staying in sector $X$, and (2) leaving sector $X$, waiting for a period of $D$, paying the additional financial adjustment cost $g'(\dot{N})$, and from then on earning $w_{y\tau} (= MP_{y\tau})$.

Thus, $NPV_{y(t+D)} - g'(\dot{N}) = NPV_{xt}$ is the condition for the equilibrium rate of transfer of labor. Let us examine this condition by, first, expressing it explicitly:

$$(4.15) \qquad \int_{t+D}^{\infty} MP_{y\tau} e^{-r(\tau-t)} d\tau - g'(\dot{N}) = \int_{t}^{\infty} MP_{x\tau} P_{x\tau} e^{-r(\tau-t)} d\tau.$$

Second, add

$$\int_{t}^{t+D} MP_{y\tau} e^{-r(\tau-t)} d\tau$$

to both sides of equation (4.15) and rearrange to obtain:

$$(4.16) \qquad \int_{t}^{t+D} MP_{y\tau} e^{-r(\tau-t)} d\tau + g'(\dot{N})$$

$$= \int_{t}^{\infty} (MP_{y\tau} - MP_{x\tau} P_{x\tau}) e^{-r(\tau-t)} d\tau.$$

Comparison of equations (4.7') and (4.17), which follows, leads to the important conclusion that, in the model postulated in case A, the marginal adjustment costs are the sum of the net present value of the wages foregone in sector $Y$ because of the waiting period and any additional financial adjustment costs $g'(\dot{N})$:

$$(4.17) \qquad \phi'(\dot{N}) = \int_{t}^{t+D} w_{y\tau} e^{-r(\tau-t)} d\tau + g'(\dot{N}).$$

Furthermore, the equilibrium rate of transfer of labor implied by equation (4.16) is the same as that expressed in equation (4.2) which is the socially optimal rate.

Now let us introduce a system, as in case B, where benefits are usually charged partially to workers' previous employers in sector $X$. The firm's layoff decision can be presented formally as follows. The present value at time $t$ ($PVB_D$) of the weekly unemployment benefits received by a laid-off worker is

$$(4.18) \quad PVB_D = \int_{t}^{t+D} \hat{b} e^{-r(\tau-t)} \, d\tau = (1 - e^{-rD}) \frac{\hat{b}}{r},$$

where $\hat{b}$ is the weekly benefit amount (expressed at an annual rate) and $D$ is the duration of unemployment (measured in years, so that, for example, 0.25 stands for 13 weeks). The proportion of UI benefits paid for by firms is $\theta$ (typically $0 \le \theta \le 1$). Thus, $\theta PVB_D$ represents the *marginal tax cost* of layoffs to the representative firm in the contracting sector. It depends positively on the waiting period $D$ and the weekly benefit payments $\hat{b}$ and negatively on the rate of interest $r$.

The condition for the firm's profit-maximizing layoffs is given by the equality of marginal costs and marginal benefits:

$$(4.19) \quad \theta PVB_D = \int_{t}^{\infty} (w_{x\tau} - P_{x\tau} MP_{x\tau}) e^{-r(\tau-t)} \, d\tau.$$

Is the firm's profit-maximizing layoff rate, as determined by equation (4.19), equal to the socially optimal rate of layoffs, as given by equation (4.16)? To answer this question, the wage in sector $X$, $w_x$ in equation (4.19), needs to be determined. This is done in the framework of two alternative assumptions about the working of the labor market. It is assumed, first, that markets are perfect, such that wages in sector $X$ are flexible; the second alternative is that relative wages in sector $X$ are inflexible and are equal to wages in sector $Y$, that is, $w_y$.

When the wage rates $w_{x\tau}$ in equation (4.19) are flexible, their present value must be determined by the equality of the properly discounted income streams in sectors $X$ and $Y$:

$$(4.20) \quad \int_{t}^{\infty} w_{x\tau} e^{-r(\tau-t)} \, d\tau = PVB_D + \int_{t+D}^{\infty} MP_{y\tau} e^{-r(\tau-t)} \, d\tau - g'(\dot{N}).$$

The right-hand side of equation (4.20) consists of the earnings in sector $Y$ from period $(t + D)$ onward, plus the unemployment benefits for the period $t$ to $(t + D)$, less the financial costs of transferring to sector $Y$. It is, thus, the present value of the net income earned in sector $Y$, which, in the flexible wage model, must equal the present value of the returns from staying in sector $X$, namely the left-hand side of equation (4.20). Equation (4.20) is now used to replace the present value of the earnings stream in equation (4.19), which then becomes

$$(4.21) \quad \int_{t}^{t+D} MP_{y\tau} e^{-r(\tau - t)} \, d\tau + g'(\dot{N}) - PVB_D (1 - \theta)$$

$$= \int_{t}^{\infty} (MP_{y\tau} - MP_{x\tau} P_{x\tau}) e^{-r(\tau - t)} \, d\tau .$$

In view of the definition of $PVB_D$ given in equation (4.18), the above condition can be written as

$$(4.22) \quad \int_{t}^{t+D} [MP_{y\tau} - (1 - \theta) \hat{b}] \, e^{-r(\tau - t)} \, d\tau + g'(\dot{N})$$

$$= \int_{t}^{\infty} (MP_{y\tau} - MP_{x\tau} P_{x\tau}) e^{-r(\tau - t)} \, d\tau .$$

Since $0 \leq \theta \leq 1$ and $\hat{b} < MP_y = w_y$ (unemployment benefits average around 50 to 60 percent of wages) we conclude that, with given $D$ and $\dot{N}$, the left-hand side of equation (4.22) must be *less than* that of equation (4.16). To maintain the postulated equality to the right-hand side in these two equations, $\dot{N}$ and $D$ must be higher under the conditions of equation (4.22) than under those of equation (4.16). Thus, imperfect experience rating, which occurs because $\theta < 1$, leads to nonoptimally high layoffs by firms and to levels of unemployment that are higher than optimal (caused by the lengthening of $D$).

Under the second set of conditions, the relative wages in sector $X$ are inflexible and are equal to the wages in sector $Y$, that is, $w_x = w_y = MP_y$. In this case equation (4.19) becomes

$$(4.23) \quad \theta PVB_D = \int_{t}^{\infty} (MP_{y\tau} - MP_{x\tau} P_{x\tau}) e^{-r(\tau - t)} \, d\tau .$$

Comparison of equations (4.16) and (4.23) suggests that the optimal transfer of labor from sector $X$ to sector $Y$ requires, under the current assumptions, that the marginal tax costs of layoffs, $\theta PVB_D$, be equal to the present value of $w_y$ from period $t$ to period $(t + D)$ plus any additional costs of transfer, or

$$(4.24) \quad \theta \int_{t}^{t+D} \hat{b}e^{-r(\tau - t)} d\tau = \int_{t}^{t+D} MP_{y\tau}e^{-r(\tau - t)} d\tau + g'(\dot{N}) \ .$$

Since, in practice $0 \le \theta \le 1$ and $\hat{b} < MP_y$, this equality does not hold. In other words, the profit-maximizing layoff decision implied by equation (4.23) leads to layoffs and an unemployment duration that are in excess of the socially optimal ones. Socially optimal layoffs and unemployment duration may be achieved by raising $\theta$ and/or $\hat{b}$. For that purpose, the increase in unemployment benefits $\hat{b}$ need not actually be paid to the unemployed workers. It serves to raise the marginal costs of layoffs in equation (4.23), so that the rate of layoffs and consequently the duration and level of unemployment are reduced toward their social optima.

## NOTES

1. In other chapters of this book the symbol $\tau$ has been used to denote the tax rate. Since the contexts are quite different, this should not cause any confusion.

2. Nonlabor income accrues to all other factors of production and to entrepreneurs as pure profits.

3. In this respect, the present specification differs from that of the standard search theory of unemployment, according to which unemployed workers search until they have located their reservation wage. At this point, individuals terminate the period of unemployment. In the present specification, unemployed workers take the waiting period as given, although it lengthens as the total number of transfers from sector $X$ to sector $Y$ increases.

# 5

# Financing the Costs
# of Permanent Job Losses
# Under the Reserve
# and Benefit Ratio Methods

We now turn to an investigation of how the two predominant methods of experience rating internalize the charged benefits of, and thereby affect, permanent layoffs. Permanent, unlike temporary, layoffs do entail long-run employment reductions and permanent decreases in the taxable payroll. These decreases make the ensuing analysis of the reserve and benefit ratio methods particularly complex.

First, we shall investigate the marginal tax costs of permanent layoffs when the employer is and expects to remain at either the maximum or the minimum tax rate. This analysis applies to both methods of experience rating. Second, we examine the tax costs of permanent layoffs under the reserve ratio method when employers are and expect to remain on the sloped part of the tax schedule. Third, we analyze these costs for employers who are and expect to remain on the sloped part of the benefit ratio tax schedule. We then compare the tax costs under the two methods of experience rating.

## Minimum and Maximum Tax Rates

Consider an employer whose long-run position is at the maximum tax rate under either the reserve or benefit ratio method of experience rating. The employer's tax payments are less than his/her charged benefits arising from temporary layoffs. Since the tax rate is fixed, there is no automatic way in which tax payments can be raised and brought into equality with charged benefits. Permanent layoffs will cause additional charged benefits, but, since these layoffs also reduce the taxable payroll, tax payments must fall. Hence, with increased benefits and reduced tax payments, the firm's deficit in its unemployment insurance (UI) account grows.

There is no possibility that the employer can be moved to the sloped (that is, experience-rated) part of the tax schedule. After the temporary increase in charged benefits due to the permanent layoffs, charged benefits will decline; this occurs because, with a constant temporary layoff rate, the reduction in employment brings about a fall in temporary layoffs. Nevertheless, the employer will remain at the maximum tax rate.

The same reasoning applies to those employers whose long-run position is at the minimum tax rate, at which tax payments exceed charged benefits. The increase in charged benefits due to the downward adjustment of employment may drive the employer temporarily to the sloped part of the tax schedule, but, in the long run, the employer must remain at the minimum tax rate. Permanent employment reductions lead to decreases in taxable payrolls and, at the constant minimum or maximum tax rates, to reduced tax payments. This means that the marginal tax cost of permanent layoffs is negative. Employers receive a tax reward for permanently laying off employees.

Let us elaborate upon the preceding analysis using the notation of chapter 2. The employer's long-run position at the maximum tax rate ($\tau_{\text{MAX}}$) is characterized by the following inequality: $\tau_{\text{MAX}} \hat{w} N^* \leq buN^*$, where $N^*$ is the initial level of employment, $\hat{w}$ is the taxable wage base (so that $\hat{w} N^*$ is the taxable payroll), $b$ measures the benefits paid per unemployment spell, and $u$ is the temporary layoff rate (so that $buN^*$ represents the charged benefits). All variables refer to the employer's long-run position.

Suppose now that $\Delta N$ employees are laid off permanently and that the new long-run level of employment is $N^{**}$ (or $N^* - \Delta N$). During the downward adjustment from $N^*$ to $N^{**}$, charged benefits rise by $b\Delta N$ because of the permanent layoffs. Once the new long-run position is reached, however, the level of charged benefits will again be determined by temporary layoffs.

In the new long-run situation, both the tax bill and charged benefits will have fallen by the same proportion, so that benefit payments will continue to exceed taxes, or $\tau_{\text{MAX}} \hat{w} N^{**} \leq buN^{**}$. In other words, changes in the level of long-run employment cannot turn an excess of benefits over taxes into a shortfall. Hence, these changes cannot move the employer to the sloped part of the tax schedule. Such a move can only be achieved by increases in $\tau_{MAX}$ and $\hat{w}$ or by decreases in $b$ and $u$.

A numerical example may be helpful. Suppose that, in the initial long run, the taxable wage base $\hat{w}$ is \$7,000, the maximum tax rate $\tau_{MAX}$ is 6 percent, the average unemployment benefit $b$ per (temporary) layoff spell is \$3,000, the temporary layoff rate $u$ is 15 percent, and the beginning level of employment $N^*$ is 100. This means that, in the initial long run, the employer's tax payments are $T^*=$ (\$7,000) (0.06) (100) = \$42,000, and the charged benefits are $CB^*=$ (\$3,000) (0.15) (100) = \$45,000. Thus, the charged benefits exceed the tax payments.

Suppose now that the employer permanently lays off 10 employees. This leads to a short-run increase in benefits of (10) (\$3,000) = \$30,000. In the new long run, however, both taxes and benefits are lower by 10 percent, namely $T^{**}=$ (\$7,000) (0.06) (90) = \$37,800, and $CB^{**}=$ (\$3,000) (0.15) (90) = \$40,500. Changes in employment cannot convert a deficit into a surplus, but they do affect the size of the deficit.

A very similar argument is relevant to an employer whose long-run position is at $\tau_{MIN}$, where tax payments exceed the benefit flows, or $\tau_{MIN}\hat{w} N^* \geq buN^*$. As before, a permanent reduction in the long-run level of employment from $N^*$ to $N^{**}$ causes a temporary increase of $b\Delta N$ in charged benefits. However, in the new long run, both taxes and benefit payments must fall in the same proportion, and the employer's excess of taxes over benefits cannot be changed into a shortfall. Because of the short-run increase in benefits, the employer may move temporarily from $\tau_{MIN}$ to $\tau_{SLOPE}$, but, in the new long run, the employer must return to $\tau_{MIN}$. Only decreases in $\tau_{MIN}$ and $\hat{w}$ or increases in $b$ and $u$ can shift the employer permanently to the sloped part of the tax schedule.

Consider now the marginal tax costs of permanent layoffs for employers who are and remain at $\tau_{MAX}$ or $\tau_{MIN}$. Their tax bills are $\tau_{MAX}\hat{w} N^*$ or $\tau_{MIN}\hat{w} N^*$, and so their marginal tax costs are $\tau_{MAX}\hat{w} \Delta N$ or $\tau_{MIN}\hat{w} \Delta N$, respectively. Since $\Delta N$ is the employment reduction, the marginal tax cost is negative. Thus, the employers receive a marginal reward for laying off workers permanently. When the taxable wage base $\hat{w}$ is \$7,000, the maximum tax rate $\tau_{MAX}$ is 6 percent, and the minimum tax rate $\tau_{MIN}$ is 0.5 percent, then the annual tax reward for laying off an employee is \$420 and \$35 for employers who are at $\tau_{MAX}$ and $\tau_{MIN}$, respectively. The net present values of these annual amounts is likely to be quite substantial. Ironically, employers at $\tau_{\text{MIN}}$, who are net contributors to the UI fund, receive a smaller tax reward from permanent layoffs than do employers at $\tau_{\text{MAX}}$, who are net claimants.

The marginal tax costs of temporary layoffs have been found to be zero for employers who are located permanently at $\tau_{\text{MAX}}$ or $\tau_{\text{MIN}}$.[1] For permanent layoffs, our analysis in this section shows that the marginal tax costs are negative and that they vary inversely with the taxable wage base $\hat{w}$ and the tax rate, $\tau_{\text{MAX}}$ or $\tau_{\text{MIN}}$. Thus, the marginal tax costs will differ from state to state.

## The Reserve Ratio Method of Experience Rating

We now turn our attention to those employers whose long-run position is on the sloped part of the tax schedule and examine, first of all, the reserve ratio method of experience rating. We postulate that the employer's UI account is initially in a steady state, which means that the balance does not change through time. (This balance has already been defined in chapter 2, equation (2.3).) Its stability implies a reserve ratio and tax rate such that an employer's tax payments have been brought into equality with charged benefits. For a steady state to emerge, the level of employment, the temporary layoff rate, and the parameters of the UI system have to remain constant for at least five calendar years. This is implied by the lags in the reserve ratio method described in chapter 2.

In the steady state, the employers' balances depend on their level of employment. If the initial steady state balance is positive, then it rises and falls equiproportionately with the level of employment. Thus, a permanent reduction in employment of $x$ percent leads to a decrease in the steady state balance of $x$ percent. The decline in the balance, in turn, implies that total charged benefits must exceed total tax payments during the period of adjustment: under the reserve ratio method of experience rating, any excess of charged benefits over tax payments is financed by a reduction in the employer's balance.

Consequently, the difference between the steady state balances before and after the employment reduction measures the cumulative excess of charged benefits over tax payments. Employers need not pay for all the charged benefits caused by the permanent layoffs because the reserve ratio method allows them to draw down their balances in the UI account. This situation is the basic reason why there cannot be complete experience rating of the charged benefits attributable to permanent layoffs. Since we know the charged benefits caused by permanent layoffs and the gap between cumulative charged benefits and tax payments, we are able to compute a marginal tax cost of permanent layoffs. These costs are less than the marginal tax costs of temporary layoffs.

The preceding arguments can be presented in the formal terms of equations (2.3) to (2.5) in chapter 2. The employer's steady state balance ($B^*$) occurs when tax payments ($T$) equal charged benefits ($CB$). Thus, according to equation (2.3), when $T_t = CB_t$ for at least three calendar years, then $B_t = B_{t-1} = B_{t-2} = B^*$. This requires that the level of employment ($N$), the rate of temporary layoffs ($u$), the benefits per unemployment spell ($b$), the taxable wage base ($\hat{w}$), the intercept ($a$) of the tax schedule, and the slope ($s$) of the tax schedule have all been constant for at least five calendar years. In that case, the tax bill for year $t$ can be written as

$$(5.1) \quad T^* = \tau \hat{w} N^* = a \hat{w} N^* - s B^*,$$

where $N^*$ is the initial steady state level of employment. As before, the level of charged benefits is

$$(5.2) \quad CB^* = b u N^*.$$

The equality of tax payments and charged benefits implies that

$$(5.3) \quad a \hat{w} N^* - s B^* = b u N^*,$$

which can be solved for the steady state level of the employer's balance:

$$(5.4) \quad B^* = \frac{1}{s} (a \hat{w} - b u) N^*.$$

This equation shows that the initial steady state balance is affected positively by increases in $a$ and $\hat{w}$ and negatively by increases in $s$, $b$, and *u*. In our subsequent discussion, the influence of changes in the steady state level of employment $N^*$ will be especially important. The impact of such changes on $B^*$ is positive if $a\hat{w} > bu$ and negative if $a\hat{w} < bu$. The inequality $a\hat{w} < bu$ implies, however, that the employer has a negative steady state balance. According to the laws of most states, employers with negative balances, and therefore negative reserve ratios, are usually assigned the maximum tax rate ($\tau_{MAX}$). Thus, employers on the sloped part of the tax schedule can be presumed to have positive balances. We consequently assume for the remainder of this chapter that $a\hat{w} > bu$, so that changes in $N^*$ affect $B^*$ positively.

Although the employer's steady state balance is influenced by the level of employment, note that both the steady state reserve ratio and the steady state tax rate are independent of the level of employment. The steady state reserve ratio is $RR^* = B^*/\hat{w} N^*$, which, in turn, equals $(a - bu/\hat{w})/s$. The steady state tax rate is $\tau^* = ub/\hat{w}$. It follows that employment changes cannot drive the steady state solution to $\tau_{MAX}$ or $\tau_{MIN}$ if the employer's steady state reserve ratio and tax rate are on the sloped part of the tax schedule.

It has been shown that the dynamic system represented by equations (2.3), (2.4), and (2.5) is stable if $\underline{RR} \leq RR^* \leq \overline{RR}$ and if $0 < s < 1$.[2] When these conditions are satisfied, and if $N$ and all the parameters of the system have been constant through time, then $RR$, $\tau$, and $B$ will converge to $RR^*$, $\tau^*$, and $B^*$, no matter whether the firm starts from $\tau_{MAX}$, $\tau_{SLOPE}$, or $\tau_{MIN}$. The movement toward the steady state is achieved by the adjustment of the tax rate and, thus, the tax bill to bring the latter into equality with charged benefits. If initially $T > CB$, then $\tau$ and $T$ fall. On the other hand, if initially, $T < CB$, then $\tau$ and $T$ rise.

We now postulate that there is a hypothetical employer whose UI finance account is in a steady state on the sloped part of the tax schedule. This initial steady state, with its employment level of $N^*$, is disturbed by permanent layoffs of $\Delta N$, which reduce the level of employment to $N^{**}$ (where $N^{**} = N^* - \Delta N$, so that $\Delta N$ is a positive number). During the downsizing, the employer's charged benefits rise by $b\Delta N$, but they decline thereafter because, with a constant temporary layoff rate, the level of these layoffs must fall with the level of employment. After $m$ years, the employer's account is in a new steady state; here tax payments again equal charged benefits, and the reserve ratio and the tax rate are the same as in the initial steady state (that is, $R^{**} =$

$R^*$, and $\tau^{**} = \tau^*$). Consequently, the new steady state must again be on the sloped part of the tax schedule. However, the employer's steady state balance has fallen to $B^{**}$, where $B^{**} < B^*$.

During the period of adjustment from $B^*$ to $B^{**}$, total charged benefits must exceed total tax payments. The deficit is financed by and must be exactly equal to the reduction in the balance. Thus, the amount of the deficit is

$$(5.5) \qquad B^* - B^{**} = \sum_{t-m}^{t} CB_{t-i} - \sum_{t-m}^{t} T_{t-i}$$

which, according to equation (5.4), must be equal to

$$(5.6) \qquad B^* - B^{**} = \frac{1}{s}(a\hat{w} - bu)\,\Delta N .$$

According to equations (5.4) and (5.6), the larger the intercept $a$ of the tax schedule and the taxable wage base $\hat{w}$, the larger the cumulative shortfall of tax inflows will be. Also, the smaller the slope $s$ of the tax schedule and the per-employee charged benefits due to temporary layoffs $bu$, the larger will be the cumulative shortfall of tax inflows.

Since the charged benefits due to permanent layoffs are $b\Delta N$ and the tax shortfall is given by equation (5.6), we can compute the marginal tax costs as the difference between the charged benefits and the tax shortfall. In other words, if the charged benefits are not financed by a reduction in the balance, then they must be paid via increased taxes. Consequently, the marginal tax costs of permanent layoffs are as follows:

$$(5.7) \qquad \text{Marginal Tax Costs of Permanent Layoffs}$$

$$= \left[ b - \frac{1}{s}(a\hat{w} - bu) \right] \Delta N .$$

If the employer's balance is positive, so that $a\hat{w} > bu$, the marginal tax cost is always less than the charged benefits caused by permanent layoffs. Equation (5.7) implies that the marginal tax cost tends to rise with the benefit rate $b$, the temporary layoff rate $u$, and the slope $s$ of the tax schedule and to fall with increases in the intercept $a$ of the tax schedule and the taxable wage base $\hat{w}$.

An arithmetic example may be helpful. Suppose that the intercept a of the tax schedule is 0.07, the slope $s$ is 0.25, the taxable wage base $\hat{w}$ is \$7,000, the temporary layoff rate $u$ is 0.10, and the benefits per unemployment spell $b$ amount to \$2,500. Then, according to equation (5.6), for every laid-off employee, tax inflows must fall short of benefit outflows during the adjustment period by an amount equal to [(0.07) (7,000) - (0.10) 2,500)]/0.25 = 960. Thus, if the firm is charged the full \$2,500 for a laid-off worker, its taxes will increase by only \$1,540; the proportionate marginal tax cost is 61.6 percent. The remaining \$960 is financed by a reduction in the firm's balance.

The discussion so far has been couched in terms of the sum of the undiscounted tax shortfalls over the period of adjustment. This corresponds to the present reserve ratio method of experience rating and is equivalent to assuming a zero interest rate. Since benefits to permanently laid-off employees are paid in period $(t + 1)$ but increases in tax payments begin only in period $(t + 3)$, a positive rate of interest induces rational employers to discount future tax liabilities back to period $(t + 1)$. This discounting reduces the present value of future tax liabilities and increases any tax shortfall. As the tax shortfall increases, the marginal tax costs of layoffs must fall. Discounting by employers will reduce the value of the marginal tax cost given by equation (5.7) and in the numerical example of the previous paragraph.

It should be pointed out that the undiscounted tax shortfall, equal to the decline in the steady state balance, is the same whether or not the tax rate is constrained by $\tau_{MAX}$ during the period of adjustment. Since $RR^{**} = RR^{*}$ lies on the sloped part of the tax schedule, the firm must eventually return to the initial $\tau_{SLOPE}$. When the unconstrained reserve ratio method generates a tax rate in excess of $\tau_{MAX}$, the constraint reduces tax payments and thus decreases the growth of the reserve ratio. Since the reserve ratio method has an infinitely long memory, a binding $\tau_{MAX}$ increases the period over which the adjustment takes place, but it does not affect the total undiscounted tax shortfall. The lower the $\tau_{MAX}$, however, the later will tax payments be made; thus, the sum of the discounted tax shortfall decreases with a decline in $\tau_{MAX}$.

Cook (1992) found that the marginal tax cost of temporary layoffs is equal to $b\Delta N$ for employers at $\tau_{SLOPE}$ facing a zero rate of interest. Hence, employers whose steady state position is on the sloped part of the tax schedule are completely experience rated when the rate of interest is zero. Similar results have been obtained by other researchers. Our results show that the same conclusion does not hold for permanent lay-offs. If employers have positive balances in their UI account, then the marginal tax cost of permanent layoffs is less than $b\Delta N$, even if the rate of interest is zero. This result seems not to have been treated before in the literature.[3]

In the preceding analysis, it has been assumed that the employer puts no value on the reduction of his/her account balance due to perma-nent layoffs. Costs arise only from taxes. This assumption appears to be realistic in the present institutional framework, in which the employer's balance is simply a convenient accounting device. If the employer could be made to value fully the reduction in the balance, then the tax shortfall would disappear and the marginal (tax plus bal-ance) costs of permanent layoffs would be equal to charged benefits. In chapter 6, these ideas are developed further and lead to the policy pro-posals that interest be paid on balances and that employers be given limited opportunities to dispose of their balances.

There is one other interesting result of the foregoing discussion of the reserve ratio method of experience rating. Equation (5.6) implies that the tax shortfall when employment declines, measured by the change in the balance, would be precisely equal to the tax surplus when employment rises by an equal amount. In other words, under the reserve ratio method, tax payments exactly equal charged benefits over a complete employment cycle. Similarly, when some employers are contracting and others are expanding, the former have a tax shortfall and the latter a tax surplus, so that the aggregate balance need not be affected much. As will be pointed out in the following section, the same situation does not hold for the benefit ratio method.

## The Benefit Ratio Method of Experience Rating

Our next step is to evaluate how the benefit ratio method works with permanent reductions in the level of employment. For this purpose, we postulate that the UI account of the hypothetical employer is in an ini-tial "steady state," in which the relevant variables have been constant for at least five calendar years, so that neither the firm's charged benefits nor its tax payments vary through time.[4] It is not necessary here, however, for tax payments to equal charged benefits.

The initial steady state is disturbed by permanent layoffs. After five calendar years, a new steady state is established, with a lower level of employment. All the other relevant variables have remained the same. The question that we wish to answer is the following: Over the five-year period, by how much have taxes increased in response to the charged benefits attributable to the permanent layoffs?

Two opposing factors affect the charged benefits over the period of adjustment. First, permanent layoffs raise charged benefits; second, with a constant temporary layoff rate, the lower permanent level of employment reduces the level of charged benefits. Hence, when cumulated over five years, charged benefits may either rise or fall. The higher the temporary layoff rate, the more likely the fall in cumulative charged benefits.

Tax payments are also subject to two opposing forces. The decline in the level of employment leads to an immediate reduction in the taxable payroll and consequently to a fall in tax liabilities. On the other hand, any increase in charged benefits may lead to a rise in the tax rate. The net outcome cannot be determined theoretically, but, with plausible assumptions about the relevant parameter values, the cumulative tax payments will fall.

As before, the net tax shortfall is defined as the difference between the cumulative charged benefits and the cumulative tax payments. We have found that, in general, the tax shortfall may be positive or negative under the benefit ratio method of experience rating and is crucially dependent upon the slope of the tax function. When this slope is close to unity, as it is in most states, the tax shortfall is definitely positive: cumulative tax payments are insufficient to pay for the increased charged benefits caused by permanent layoffs.

The marginal tax cost of a permanent layoff is less than that of a temporary layoff under the benefit ratio method of experience rating, as is true under the reserve ratio method. There are significant differences between the tax costs of temporary and of permanent layoffs.

We will now derive these results in the framework of the model of the benefit ratio method presented in chapter 2. Assume that the employer's UI account is in a steady state, which requires that the variables $\hat{w}$, $N^*$, $u$, $b$, $c$, and $k$ have been constant for at least five years. As in chapter 2, $c$ is the intercept, and $k$ is the slope of the tax schedule. The charged benefits amount to $CB^* = ubN^*$, the benefit ratio is $BR^* = ub/\hat{w}$, and, assuming that the firm is on the sloped part of the tax schedule (that is, as in figure 2.2, $\underline{BR} < BR^* < \overline{BR}$), the tax rate is $\tau_{SLOPE}^* = c + kBR^*$. Consequently, the employer's tax bill in the initial steady state is equal to

(5.8)    $T^* = c\hat{w}N^* + kubN^*$.

When $c = 0$ and $k = 1$, then $T^* = CB^* = ubN^*$; that is, tax payments equal charged benefits.

The initial steady state is now disturbed. At the end of year $t$, the firm permanently lays off $\Delta N$ workers, who receive unemployment benefits in year $(t + 1)$. The new permanent level of employment is $N^{**} = N^* - \Delta N$. At the beginning of year $(t + 6)$ the firm reaches a new steady state. The new charged benefits are $CB^{**} = ub(N^* - \Delta N) = CB^* - ub\Delta N$. The steady state benefit ratio, by contrast, is independent of the level of employment and remains at $BR^{**} = BR^* = ub/\hat{w}$. The equality of the two steady state benefit ratios implies that the two steady state tax rates are also equal to one another (that is, $\tau_{SLOPE}^{**} = \tau_{SLOPE}^*$). Thus, the new steady state tax bill is equal to

(5.9)    $T^{**} = c\hat{w}(N^* - \Delta N) + kub(N^* - \Delta N)$.

This means that the permanent drop in the level of employment lowers the tax liability by $T^* - T^{**} = \Delta N(c\hat{w} + kub)$, which reduces to $T^* - T^{**} = ub\Delta N$ when $c = 0$ and $k = 1$. The reason for the decline in the tax liability is that, with a constant temporary layoff rate, the reduction in employment causes a fall in temporary layoffs.

In years $(t + 1)$ to $(t + 5)$, the firm's tax liability adjusts from the first to the second steady state level. In year $(t + 1)$, charged benefits rise by $b\Delta N$ because of permanent layoffs and fall by $\Delta Nub$ because of reduced temporary layoffs, so that the net increase is $b\Delta N(1 - u)$. In years $(t + 2)$, $(t + 3)$, $(t + 4)$, and $(t + 5)$, charged benefits are below their initial steady state level by an amount equal to $ub\Delta N$. This means that the sum of the (undiscounted) additional charged benefits over the entire five years equals

$$(5.10) \quad \sum_{i=1}^{5} (CB_{t+i} - CB^*) = b(1 - 5u)\,\Delta N.$$

As previously stated, when summed over the five years of transition, charged benefits may rise or fall. The larger the temporary layoff rate, the more probable the fall in charged benefits.

What happens to taxes during the adjustment period? Assume initially that the firm remains on the sloped part of the tax schedule throughout the adjustment period, i.e., that $\tau_t < \tau_{MAX}$ at all times. As specified in chapter 2, the tax rate reacts to changes in the benefit ratio with a two-year lag. This means that the tax rates for the years $(t + 1)$ and $(t + 2)$ are the same as in the initial steady state $(\tau_{t+1} = \tau_{t+2} = \tau_{SLOPE}^*)$. Because of the decline in the taxable payroll, however, the tax payments in these years must fall. These changes can be easily ascertained as

$$(5.11) \quad T_{t+1} - T^* = -(c\hat{w} + kub)\,\Delta N \text{ and}$$

$$(5.12) \quad T_{t+2} - T^* = -(c\hat{w} + kub)\,\Delta N.$$

The derivation of the changes in the tax bill for the years $(t + 3)$, $(t + 4)$, and $(t + 5)$ is straightforward but tedious. If the firm does not reach $\tau_{MAX}$ during the adjustment period, the changes are as follows:

$$(5.13) \quad T_{t+3} - T^* = -\left[c\hat{w} + bk\left(u - \frac{N^{**}}{2N^* + N^{**}}\right)\right]\Delta N,$$

$$(5.14) \quad T_{t+4} - T^* = -\left[c\hat{w} + bk\left(u - \frac{N^{**}}{2N^{**} + N^*}\right)\right]\Delta N, \text{ and}$$

$$(5.15) \quad T_{t+5} - T^* = -\left[c\hat{w} + bk\left(u - \frac{1}{3}\right)\right]\Delta N.$$

The sum of the (undiscounted) changes in the tax bill is equal to

$$(5.16) \quad \sum_{i=1}^{5} (T_{t+i} - T^*) = -[5c\hat{w} - bk(\delta - 5u)\,]\Delta N,$$

where

(5.17) $\quad \delta = \dfrac{N^{**\cdot\cdot}}{N^{**\cdot} + 2N^*} + \dfrac{N^{**\cdot}}{2N^{**\cdot} + N^*} + \dfrac{1}{3}.$

Since $N^{**} < N^*$, it can readily be shown that $\delta$ in equation (5.17) must be less than unity (i.e., that $\delta < 1$). Further, it is easy to show that $\delta$ falls as the relative difference between $N^*$ and $N^{**}$ increases.

In order to ascertain any possible tax shortfall, we simply deduct equation (5.16) from equation (5.10):

(5.18) $\quad \displaystyle\sum_{i=1}^{5} [\,(CB_{t+i} - CB^*) - (T_{t+i} - T^*)\,]$

$\qquad = \{5c\hat{w} + b\,[\,(1-5u) - k\,(\delta - 5u)\,]\ \}\Delta N$

This expression may be negative, which would imply that the firm's tax payments exceed its charged benefits during the years of adjustment. In practice, the slope of the tax function $k$ is usually equal to unity. In that case, equation (5.18) becomes

(5.19) $\quad \displaystyle\sum_{i=1}^{5} [\,(CB_{t+i} - CB^*) - (T_{t+i} - T^*)\,]$

$\qquad = [5c\hat{w} + b\,(1-\delta)\,]\,\Delta N.$

Now the tax shortfall is always positive.

The charged benefits arising from the permanent layoffs are equal to $b\Delta N$, and the tax shortfall is given by equation (5.18). The (undiscounted) marginal tax cost is defined as the difference between the former and the latter, namely:

(5.20) $\quad$ Marginal Tax Cost of Permanent Layoffs
$\qquad = \{b\,[5u + k\,(\delta - 5u)\,] - 5c\hat{w}\}\,\Delta N.$

Equation (5.20) implies that the larger the relative employment decline (that is, the smaller the $\delta$) and the benefit rate $b$, the larger the marginal tax cost. Also, the smaller the intercept of the tax schedule $c$ and the taxable wage base $\hat{w}$, the larger the marginal tax cost. The slope $k$ of the tax schedule and the temporary layoff rate $u$ have an uncertain impact on the marginal tax cost. When $k$ is 1, as it is in most benefit ratio states, equation (5.20) reduces to $(b\delta - 5c\hat{w})\Delta N$.

A numerical example may again be helpful. Suppose that, as before, the benefit per layoff spell is $2,500 and the interest rate is zero. If the reduction in employment is 20 percent, the intercept of the tax schedule is 0.5 percent and the taxable wage base is $7,000, then, according to equation (5.17), $\delta$ is 93 percent and the marginal tax cost of one layoff is $(b\delta - 5c\hat{w}) = [(\$2,500)(.93) - (5)(.005)(\$7,000)]$ which is equal to $2,150 or 86 percent of the charged benefits.

Cook (1992) found that under the benefit ratio method, the marginal tax cost of temporary layoffs with a zero rate of interest and a unitary slope of the tax function is equal to $b\Delta N$, which implies complete experience rating. Equation (5.20) shows that the (undiscounted) marginal tax costs of permanent layoffs are less than those of temporary layoffs for two reasons: first, $\delta < 1$, and, second, $c \geq 0$.

Equations (5.11) to (5.20) are based on the assumption that the firm does not reach $\tau_{MAX}$ during the period of adjustment from the initial to the new steady state. If this assumption is incorrect and the permanent layoffs do push the employer to $\tau_{MAX}$ temporarily, then the marginal tax costs of permanent layoffs are reduced. This result is due to the relatively short memory of the benefit ratio method: past charged benefits are soon forgotten, and the employer's tax payments are not required to account for them.

As in the case of the reserve ratio method discussed in the previous section, the marginal tax costs have been computed under the assumption that the rate of interest is zero. This is because neither system of experience rating currently incorporates a positive rate of interest. As shown in the previous section, discounted marginal tax costs fall short of undiscounted ones. They do not change the basic conclusion that the marginal tax costs of permanent layoffs are less than those of temporary layoffs.

Equation (5.19) is an expression for the tax shortfall when there is a reduction in the level of employment. What happens when employment rises? It turns out that the tax surplus caused by an employment increase of $\Delta N$ is equal to $5c\hat{w} \Delta N$. Thus, the tax surplus in an employment upswing is *less* than the tax shortfall in the downswing, so that, over a complete employment cycle, taxes must fall short of charged benefits.[5] Further, in an economy where there is no no aggregate job growth, the deficit balances of contracting employers will not be totally offset by the surplus balances of expanding employers. Thus, the benefit ratio method of experience rating lacks the completely automatic financing mechanism implied by the reserve ratio method.

## The Essential Differences Between the Two Methods

As pointed out in the second section of this chapter, the two experience rating methods are basically identical when the long-run position of the employer is on the flat parts of the tax schedule. Therefore, the present discussion is confined to those cases where the steady state reserve and benefit ratios lie on the slope of the tax schedule. The following differences between the reserve ratio and benefit ratio methods of experience rating appear to be particularly relevant to permanent layoffs.

1. Both methods of experience rating tend to generate tax shortfalls when the level of employment is reduced. This implies that the marginal tax costs of permanent layoffs are less than their charged benefits. Under the reserve ratio method, the tax shortfall is associated with and financed by a reduction in the employer's balance in the UI trust fund. Under the benefit ratio method, on the other hand, the tax shortfall is caused by the lags in the system. After a decline in employment, the current taxable payroll is less than the (recent) past taxable payroll, so that the relevant benefit ratio is too low to generate the taxes for the increased charged benefits.

The responses of the marginal tax costs to changes in the various exogenous parameters have already been described in the last two sections. For the sake of comparison, they are restated in table 5.1. The sign predictions are the same for the taxable wage base, benefits per unemployment spell, and the intercept of the tax function under both methods of experience rating. When tax costs are discounted, the sign predictions in table 5.1 do not change with the exception that the impact of $\tau_{MAX}$ is positive under the reserve ratio method.

**Table 5.1  Impact of Parameter Changes on the Undiscounted Marginal Tax Cost**

| | Experience rating method | |
|---|---|---|
| **Parameter increases** | **Reserve ratio** | **Benefit ratio** |
| Taxable wage base | – | – |
| Benefits per unemployment spell | + | + |
| Temporary layoff rate | + | 0 |
| Maximum tax rate | 0 | + |
| Relative change in employment level | 0 | – |
| Slope of tax function | + | a |
| Intercept of tax function | – | – |

a. Direction of impact is indeterminate.

2. When there is a relatively "long-run" employment cycle—that is, a decline in employment of $\Delta N$ followed after several years by an increase of $\Delta N$—then the tax shortfall in the downswing is equal to the tax surplus in the upswing under the reserve ratio method. Over the full cycle, benefit outflows equal (undiscounted) tax inflows. By contrast, under the benefit ratio method, there is a shortfall in the downswing but no tax surplus in the upswing. Consequently, the benefit ratio method implies a tax shortfall over the entire employment cycle.

3. During the period of adjustment from a high to a low long-run level of employment, the employer may temporarily reach the maximum tax rate $\tau_{MAX}$ under either method of experience rating. Under the reserve ratio method, this temporary maximum tax rate does not affect the total (undiscounted) tax shortfall. The employer will have to make up the lost taxes at a later time. By contrast, under the benefit ratio method, because of its short memory, the tax shortfall is never offset. Hence, the lower the binding $\tau_{MAX}$, the larger the tax shortfall.

## Summary and Conclusions

In this chapter, we have examined the extent to which the two methods of experience rating internalize the costs of permanent layoffs. We have concluded that neither method internalizes these costs completely, even when the employer's account is placed on the slope of the tax schedule. This result is different from those obtained for temporary layoffs by other researchers. When the firm is always on the slope of the tax schedule, both methods of experience rating typically internalize all the (undiscounted) charged benefits of temporary layoffs but only part of the charged benefits of permanent layoffs.

The two experience-rating methods react differently to these conditions because the tax base, namely, the taxable payroll, remains constant with temporary layoffs, but declines with permanent layoffs. The decline in the taxable payroll reduces the tax bill and thus counteracts the rise in the tax rate due to the increase in charged benefits. Thus, payroll taxes are not the ideal means of internalizing the charged benefits of permanent layoffs.

When the firm is and remains at the maximum or the minimum tax rate, it receives a tax reward for laying off workers permanently and has a zero tax cost of temporary layoffs. Hence, our research supports the frequently made recommendation of increased maximum tax rates and decreased minimum tax rates: the tax costs of temporary layoffs would rise and the tax rewards for permanent layoffs would fall for those employers who are moved from the flat to the sloped section of the tax schedule.

We next consider which method of experience rating is superior in internalizing the charged benefits of permanent layoffs. Simple arithmetic examples have shown that realistic parameters values lead to (undiscounted) marginal tax costs that are somewhat higher for the benefit ratio than for the reserve ratio method. Nevertheless, we regard the reserve ratio method as superior for two reasons. First, when the steady state tax rate is on the slope of the tax schedule, the change in the employer's UI account balance measures the tax shortfall under the reserve ratio method. Thus, if employers can be made to value fully their balances, then complete internalization of charged benefits would occur. Second, as indicated before, both methods of experience rating suffer from the shortcoming that future tax payments are not discounted. This can be remedied easily in the case of the reserve ratio method, simply by paying interest on positive balances and charging interest on negative balances. Under the benefit ratio method, by contrast, there is no balance, so that neither of these two changes could be effected.

## NOTES

1. See, for example, Card and Levine (1994) or our own discussion in chapter 2.

2. See Brechling (1977).

3. There is an inconsistency in the empirical work of Card and Levine (1992). They use their estimates of the marginal costs of temporary layoffs in equations for permanent layoffs. Since the marginal tax costs of permanent layoffs are less than those of temporary layoffs, their tax cost coefficients for permanent layoffs are likely to have a downward bias.

4. We use the term "steady state" somewhat loosely here to describe simple constancy through time. Usually the term is used in truly dynamic systems in which at least one variable depends on its own value in a previous period. The benefit ratio method is essentially static but with lags, so that the endogenous variables depend only on the exogenous ones from the current and previous periods.

5. The technical reason why the tax surplus in the upswing is less than the tax shortfall in the downswing is that permanent layoffs qualify for UI benefits but there are no equivalent positive contributions on behalf of new permanent hires.

# 6
# Policy Recommendations for Improving Unemployment Insurance Financing

The experience-rating provisions of unemployment insurance (UI) financing are designed to internalize in part the costs of unemployment to the employer, who is the proximate cause of the job loss. These provisions imply incentives to firms to reduce layoffs and, hence, unemployment. Empirical research has shown that the incentives of experience rating may be sufficiently powerful to decrease layoffs substantially.

## Summary

In this study, we have examined the nature and working of experience rating in the U.S. UI system, which, as previously discussed, is distinctive in being financed by an experience-rated payroll tax. Most previous research in this area has been concerned with temporary layoffs, which are responses to temporary fluctuation in the demand for labor and do not require any structural adjustment. For temporary layoffs, UI provides the important service of income support. Our primary emphasis in this book, by contrast, has been on the costs of permanent layoffs or job losses that involve the contraction of some sectors of the economy and the expansion of others. Specifically, we have asked the following three questions:
1. How important are permanent in relation to temporary layoffs?
2. Who should bear the costs of permanent layoffs?
3. How do current methods of experience rating internalize these costs to employers?
We have attempted to answer these questions in chapters 3, 4, and 5, respectively.

Our basic findings are as follows. First, our empirical work suggests that permanent layoffs may constitute as much as 70 percent of all layoffs. Consequently, we believe that there is a valid rationale for examining experience rating and its effects on permanent layoffs.

Second, to obtain a socially optimal rate of structural adjustment, the agents who pay for the adjustment costs should also control the rate of adjustment. This rules out government financing from general revenues. Further, payment by employers in the expanding sectors cannot be administered. Payment by dismissed workers may work well if wages are flexible and capital markets are perfect. Payment by employers in the contracting sectors is likely to work even if wages are inflexible. Hence, there is a strong *prima facie* case for experience rating in the case of permanent layoffs.

Third, the charged benefits caused by permanent layoffs cannot be fully experience rated under either the reserve ratio or the benefit ratio method. This contrasts with the results obtained for temporary layoffs. When employers are on the sloped parts of the tax schedules, the (undiscounted) marginal tax costs of temporary layoffs are equal to charged benefits. The marginal tax costs of permanent layoffs, on the other hand, are less than the charged benefits. When employers are at the maximum and minimum tax rates, the marginal tax costs of temporary layoffs are zero and those of permanent layoffs are negative. In other words, at these tax rates employers receive a tax reward for permanent layoffs. As discussed in chapter 5, the difference between the effects of temporary and permanent layoffs is due to the declines in the tax base that occur only in the case of permanent layoffs.


## Policy Implications

Our policy implications are based on the premise that an increased degree of internalization of the costs of unemployment is desirable and that the present institutional and legal structure cannot be changed radically. Our policy findings are both "old" and "new."

Many other researchers have come to the conclusion that the maximum tax rate ought to be raised under either method of experience rating. Our research supports this view. As a result, our first policy recommendation is the following: *Maximum tax rates should be raised substantially or even be eliminated. Minimum tax rates should be reduced or even be eliminated.*

Under both methods of experience rating, there are substantial time lags between the payment of unemployment benefits and the resulting changes in taxes. In the absence of discounting, these lags undermine the working of experience rating. They result in interest-free loans to employers with high and rising charged benefits. We therefore recommend that *the administrative lag in the determination of the employer's tax rate be reduced to a minimum.* Modern computing systems should allow the 1995 tax rate, for example, to be based on the reserve or benefit ratio at the end of 1994.

From many points of view, the differences between the reserve ratio and the benefit ratio methods of experience rating are not substantial. However, we favor the reserve ratio method of experience rating because it appears to be more readily adaptable to relatively minor changes that would increase its efficiency in internalizing the costs of unemployment. The reserve ratio method is superior in this respect as it is based on the firm's balance, which is a summary of previous charged benefits and tax payments. The benefit ratio method has no such summary.

Under the reserve ratio method, the decline in the employer's balance measures the tax shortfall due to permanent layoffs when the employer's long-run (steady state) position is on the slope of the tax schedule and any movements to the maximum or minimum rate are temporary. Thus, if the employer could be made to value fully the decline in the balance, full experience rating would occur. We present three policy recommendations designed to induce employers to place an appropriate value on their trust fund balance.

1. *An employer's positive balance in the UI trust fund should be treated as part of the employer's assets; a negative balance should be treated as a liability.* The inclusion of positive and negative UI balances in the balance sheet would improve it as a reflection of employers' true financial status.

2. *Upon cessation of business, due to bankruptcy, for example, an employer's positive balance should be refunded, and any negative balance should be payable in full.* Business closures have

been a troublesome issue for the UI system. When an employer goes out of business and lays off the entire work force, the taxable payroll falls to zero and, as a result, the (payroll) tax liabilities disappear. However, the former employees qualify for and receive unemployment benefits. At present, the UI system cannot claim part of the employer's remaining assets for the reimbursement of the UI benefits. The UI system should be allowed to lay claim to the remaining assets to cover any negative balances. Similarly, any positive balance should be returned to the owners.

3. *Interest should be paid on positive balances and charged on negative balances.* The states' UI trust funds receive interest from the federal government, and it seems fair and proper that interest be paid by the trust funds to employers with positive balances. Further, interest should be charged to employers with negative balances. Interest on negative balances, however, should be cash charges and not be added to negative balances. Positive interest payments should be added to the positive balance.

Interest payments on positive and negative balances are important for at least two reasons. They give an inducement to employers, first, to avoid negative balances, and second, to build up positive ones. Typically, charged benefits occur now, and the corresponding taxes occur several years afterwards. At present, the system does not account for this difference by discounting future tax liabilities. A simple way of resolving the discounting problem under the reserve ratio method of experience rating is to pay (charge) interest on positive (negative) balances. No such simple method of dealing with the discounting problem seems to exist under the benefit ratio method.

# References

Adams, James D. 1986. "Equilibrium Taxation and Experience Rating in a Federal System of Unemployment Insurance," *Journal of Public Economics* 19: 51-77. 1986.

Anderson, Patricia M., and Bruce D. Meyer. 1994. "The Extent and Consequences of Job Turnover," *Brookings Papers on Economic Activity—Microeconomics 1994:* 177-248.

Baily, Martin N. 1977. "On the Theory of Layoffs and Unemployment," *Econometrica* 45 (July): 1043-1063.

_____. 1978. "Some Aspects of Optimal Unemployment Insurance," *Journal of Public Economics* 10 (December): 379-402.

Becker, Joseph M. 1972. *Experience Rating in Unemployment Insurance: An Experiment in Competitive Socialism.* Baltimore: Johns Hopkins University Press.

_____. 1981. *Unemployment Insurance Financing: An Evaluation.* Washington, DC: American Enterprise Institute for Public Policy Research.

Brechling, Frank. 1977. "The Incentive Effects of the U.S. Unemployment Insurance Tax." In *Research in Labor Economics*, vol. 1, 41-102, Ronald G. Ehrenberg, ed. Greenwich, CT: JAI Press.

_____. 1981. "Layoffs and Unemployment Insurance." In *Studies in Labor Markets*, 187-207, Sherwin Rosen, ed. Chicago: University of Chicago Press.

Burtless, Gary. 1990. *Unemployment Insurance and Labor Supply; A Survey.* Brookings Technical Series Reprint. Washington, DC: Brookings Institution.

Card, David, and Philip B. Levine. 1994. "Unemployment Insurance Taxes and the Cyclical and Seasonal Properties of Unemployment," *Journal of Public Economics* 53 (January): 1-29.

Clark, Kim B., and Lawrence H. Summers. 1982. "Unemployment Insurance and Labor Market Transitions." In *Workers, Jobs, and Inflation*, Martin N. Baily, ed. Washington, DC: Brookings Institution.

Cook, Zena. 1992. "Experience Rating Methods in United States Unemployment Insurance." Ph.D. dissertation, George Washington University.

Crosslin, Robert L., James S. Hanna, and David W. Stevens. 1986. "Earnings Losses and the Permanence of Dislocation: 1979-83 Evidence." Paper prepared for the National Commission for Employment Policy, Washington, DC (June).

Deere, D.R. 1991. "Unemployment Insurance and Employment," *Journal of Labor Economics* 9 (October): 307-324.

103

Feldstein, Martin. 1973. "Unemployment Compensation: Adverse Incentive and Distributional Anomalies." *National Tax Journal,* 27 (June): 231-244.

_____. 1976. "Temporary Layoffs in the Theory of Unemployment," *Journal of Political Economy,* 84 (October): 937-957.

Feldstein, Martin. 1978. "The Effect of Unemployment Insurance on Temporary Layoff Unemployment," *American Economic Review* 68 (December): 834-846.

Gustman, Alan L. 1982. "Analyzing the Relation of Unemployment Insurance and Unemployment." In *Research in Labor Economics,* vol. 5, 69-114, Ronald G. Ehrenberg, ed. Greenwich, CT: JAI Press.

Hall, Robert E. 1971. "Turnover in the Labor Force," *Brookings Papers on Economic Activity* 3: 709-756.

Hamermesh, Daniel S. 1977. *Jobless Pay and the Economy.* Baltimore: Johns Hopkins University Press.

_____. 1978. "Unemployment Insurance and Unemployment in the United States." In *Unemployment Insurance Global Evidence of its Effects on Unemployment,* Herbert G. Grubel and Michael A. Walker, eds. Canada: Fraser Institute.

Laurence, Louise. 1991. "How Do Firm Characteristics Affect the Subsidies Provided by the Unemployment Insurance System?" *Applied Economics* 23 (September): 1529-1534.

_____. 1993. "Winners and Losers in the Unemployment Insurance Financing Game," *Quarterly Review of Economics and Finance* (September).

Murphy, Kevin M., and Robert H. Topel. 1987. "The Evolution of Unemployment in the United States: 1968-1985," *NBER Macroeconomics Annual:* 87-128.

Rosen, Sherwin. 1977. "Comment to 'UI as Insurance for Workers' by Dale T. Mortensen." *Industrial and Labor Relations Review* 30 (July): 518-520.

_____. 1983. "Unemployment and Insurance." In *Variability of Employment, Prices, and Money,* Karl Brunner and Allan H. Meltzer, eds. Amsterdam: North Holland.

Stafford, Frank P. 1977. "More on Unemployment Insurance as Insurance," *Industrial and Labor Relations Review* 30 (July): 521-526.

Topel, Robert 1983. "On Layoffs and Unemployment Insurance," *American Economic Review* 73 (September): 541-549.

Topel, Robert, and Finis Welch. 1980 "Unemployment Insurance: Survey and Extensions," *Economica,* 47 (August): 351-379.

U.S. Department of Labor. *Employment and Training Handbook* 394: 476.

Wolcowitz, Jeffrey. 1984. "Dynamic Effects of the UI Tax on Temporary Layoffs." *Journal of Public Economics* 25 (November): 35-51.

# INDEX

Adams, James D., 17
Adjustment of labor transfer
  cost function, 65
  costs, 50-51, 58-62
  socially optimal rate, 50-51, 60-61
  socially optimal rate model, 63-79
Anderson, Patricia M., 17, 19-20, 34, 37

Baily, Martin Neil, 1, 10, 17, 33
Becker, Joseph M., 1, 17
Benefit ratio method
  differences from reserve ratio method,
    95-96
  distinct features of, 29-31
  of experience rating, 2, 5, 89-95
  states use of experience rating, 20
Benefits
  in model of unemployment insurance
    scenarios, 10-16
  relation to UI tax rates, 2
  of socially optimal rate of labor
    transfer, 3-4, 50-51
  for temporary and permanent layoffs,
    37
  *See also* Charged benefits;
    Noncharged benefits;
      Unemployment insurance (UI)
      benefits
Benefit wage ratio method, 36n3
Brechling, Frank, 1, 2, 17, 19, 21, 33
Burtless, Gary, 10

Card, David, 19, 34
Charged benefits
  definition and source, 22
  with permanent layoffs, 81-82
  relation to tax rate, 81
  under reserve and benefit ratio
    experience rating, 22-24
  under reserve and benefit ratio
    methods, 30-32

with time lagged employer tax rate,
  23-24
Clark, Kim B., 19
Coinsurance, 9
Cook, Zena, 2, 18, 33, 88, 94
Costs
  of adjustment of labor transfer, 3-4,
    49-50, 58-62
  employee payment of job transfer, 52-
    55, 67-72
  employer payment of worker transfer,
    55-57, 72-75
  government payment of worker
    transfer, 57-58, 75
  of internalized permanent layoff, 97
  of socially optimal rate of labor
    transfer, 3-4, 49-75
  *See also* Tax costs
Crosslin, Robert L., 37
Cross-subsidization, 17, 35

Data sources, 38
Deere, D.R., 17

Earnings
  *See* Income
Employees
  experience-rated in model of
    unemployment insurance, 14-16
  incentives, 11-13
  paying adjustment cost of job transfer,
    52-55, 67
  private insurance in model of
    unemployment insurance, 12-13, 15
  public insurance in model of
    unemployment insurance, 13-14
  self-insurance in model of
    unemployment insurance, 11-12
Employer
  as determinant of temporary or
    permanent layoff status, 22-23

105

incentives, 13, 18-19, 101-2
paying adjustment cost of worker
transfer, 55-57, 72-75
policy recommendations related to
trust funds, 101-2
reserve ratio of, 26-28
total taxable payroll, 21
Employment reductions
under benefit ratio method of
experience rating, 89-95
in growing and contracting firms, 40-
44
measurement of decline, 39-40
permanent layoffs as ratio of total
layoffs, 3
under reserve ratio method of
experience rating, 84-89
tax shortfalls under reserve and benefit
ratio
experience rating, 95
temporary and permanent, 38-40, 44-
47
Experience rating
arguments against, 18-20
of charged benefits, 84-89
circumstances for suspension of, 24,
31
conditions for changes in degrees of,
14-16, 32
federal and state guidelines for, 20
general effect and imperfections, 2-3
internalizes cost of unemployment, 1
risk class assignment in, 8
state laws governing, 25
suspension circumstances, 24
in UI temporary layoff models, 2
Experience rating methods
benefit ratio, 89-95
common features of reserve ratio and
benefit ratio methods, 20-25
distinctions and differences in reserve
and benefit ratio experience rating,
26-32
policy recommendations for reserve

ratio, 5, 101
reserve ratio, 84-89

Federal Unemployment Tax Act (FUTA),
20, 21
Feldstein, Martin, 1, 2, 17, 18, 19, 33, 37
Firms
employment changes in stable
opposed to contracting, 40-47
growing and declining, 3-4, 49, 53-63
optimal layoff levels, 33-36
tax reward for permanent layoffs, 97,
100
unemployment insurance deficits, 81-
82
*See also* Employer; Employment
reductions; Payroll tax; Tax
shifting
Free riding, 13
FUTA. *See* Federal Unemployment Tax
Act (FUTA)

Government
federal and state guidelines for UI, 20
paying adjustment costs of labor
transfer, 57-58, 75
state-level UI trust funds, 24-25
taxation, 25
Gustman, Alan L., 1

Hall, Robert E., 37
Hamermesh, Daniel S., 1
Hanna, James S., 37

Incentives
created by experience rating, 8-9, 17-
18, 99
of employer and employee with
private unemployment
insurance, 13
employer control of layoffs with
experience rating, 18-19
policy recommendations related to
employers, 101-2

# About the Institute

The W.E. Upjohn Institute for Employment Research is a nonprofit research organization devoted to finding and promoting solutions to employment-related problems at the national, state, and local level. It is an activity of the W.E. Upjohn Unemployment Trustee Corporation, which was established in 1932 to administer a fund set aside by the late Dr. W.E. Upjohn, founder of The Upjohn Company, to seek ways to counteract the loss of employment income during economic downturns.

The Institute is funded largely by income from the W.E. Upjohn Unemployment Trust, supplemented by outside grants, contracts, and sales of publications. Activities of the Institute are comprised of the following elements: (1) a research program conducted by a resident staff of professional social scientists; (2) a competitive grant program, which expands and complements the internal research program by providing financial support to researchers outside the Institute; (3) a publications program, which provides the major vehicle for the dissemination of research by staff and grantees, as well as other selected work in the field; and (4) an Employment Management Services division, which manages most of the publicly funded employment and training programs in the local area.

The broad objectives of the Institute's research, grant, and publication programs are to: (1) promote scholarship and experimentation on issues of public and private employment and unemployment policy; and (2) make knowledge and scholarship relevant and useful to policymakers in their pursuit of solutions to employment and unemployment problems.

Current areas of concentration for these programs include: causes, consequences, and measures to alleviate unemployment; social insurance and income maintenance programs; compensation; workforce quality; work arrangements; family labor issues; labor-management relations; and regional economic development and local labor markets.